VEDIC ARCHEOLOGY

and assorted essays

STEVEN ROSEN

FOLK BOOKS/ BBL

First FOLK Books Edition published in 1991 in conjunction with
Bhaktivedanta Book Trust Ltd., P.O. Box 324, Borehamwood, Herts, U.K.,
WD6 1NB. (Copies of this book and general catalog available from this
address.)

ISBN 0-9619763-5-7

For more information on the subject matter of this book contact Steven
Rosen c/o FOLK Books, P.O. Box 400716, Brooklyn, New York, 11240-
0716, U.S.A.

TABLE OF CONTENTS

GENERAL INTRODUCTION

When Amita Prabhu suggested that we reprint my *Archeology and the Vaishnava Tradition: The Pre-Christian Roots of Krishna Worship* (Calcutta, India, KLM Firma, 1989), I was a little reluctant. It was a short volume, and I doubted that it was worth the endeavor. Amita insisted, however, that we print it, and he said that we could compensate for its shortness by adding various essays that I had written over the years. "We can do an anthology," he said. "We'll call it '*Vedic Archeology and Assorted Essays.*'"

I liked the idea. But after going through dozens of my published articles—many of them poorly written—I was faced with a dilemma: which essays should I choose? I decided to look at various letters I had received over the years from people who liked certain articles and disliked others. "Let the readers decide," I thought.

So the essays included here are those most enjoyed by my readers. Other than this, there is no design to the choice of subjects or the sequence of their presentation—they are simply stray snippets and various aspects of Krishna conscious philosophy. I have tried to put them in *some* order, but the style and areas covered are too diverse.

Some are interviews; some are essays that were published with a small audience in mind; and some were published in international magazines and journals.

I have not edited these essays but have, instead, left them exactly as they appeared when they were first published. If I were writing these pieces today, I would probably render them differently. But they are presented here without change, just as the original readers appreciated them. I hope these articles offer something of lasting value to the people who peruse this volume. Most of all I hope they are pleasing to His Divine Grace A.C. Bhaktivedanta Swami Prabhupada—my spiritual master—and to my Godbrothers as well.

ARCHEOLOGY AND THE VAISHNAVA TRADITION

INTRODUCTION TO THE ORIGINAL EDITION

Those with a spiritual bent are not swayed by archeological conclusions. Having identified with the eternal soul, true spiritual seekers have little need to confirm their beliefs by poking and categorizing bones. For such souls, the archeological method is seen to have severe limitations. This work is not meant for these people. Unless, of course, these spiritual benefactors mercifully attempt to enlighten those who still enjoy a rigorous archeological debate or those who are still given to the art of mundane wrangling. In such cases this book may have some value. In addition, it may bolster the faith of an ardent Vaishnava believer.

Archeological experts themselves, however, tend to doubt the veracity of their own science. According to William Fixx, author of *The Bone Peddlers': Selling Evolution,* there is a virtual "catalogue of fiascos" in the world of archeology. Fixx attributes these errors not only to the "sincere-but-wrong." His well-documented book reveals that many archeologists and researchers are more interested in publicity, funding, and reputation than in truth. To protect their pet theories and speculations, says Fixx, researchers have deliberately ignored or dismissed evidence that detracts from their claims. Archeologists are people. And people are motivated.

But even beyond motivation, there are limits to what can be done with the archeological method. One can only dig up so many bones at a given time—one can only do so much research. Thus, archeology, like the other sciences, is always being revised. This naturally gives rise to anomalies, for just as one "fact" is being confirmed, another is being debunked. Specifics are related in Fixx's book, and these tend to make the whole archeological process questionable.

In short, people make mistakes, fall into illusion, have the propensity to cheat, and are beleagured by imperfect senses. Not only do we collect datum with these limitations, but we interpret them in the same way. Archeologists are not an exception to the rule.

The Birth Of Indology

In India, the study of archeology began as an antiquarian pursuit, thanks to the interest shown by a small group of enthusiasts who, in 1784, established the "Asiatick Society" in Calcutta. This was, in a very real sense, the birth of Indology, a study that continues to grow as knowledge of ancient languages, such as Sanskrit, continues to grow.

The first Westerner to master Sanskrit was Sir Charles Wilkins (1749-1830), who went to Bengal in 1770 as a writer and researcher for the East India Company. Soon, Wilkins assisted Sir William Jones (1746-1794), who was somewhat naively glorified as "the greatest Orientalist of the period" in learning Sanskrit. Sir Williams later declared that without the aid of Wilkins, "I should never have learned it..."[1]

In Sir Charles Wilkins' obituary, which was published in *Gentleman's Magazine* in 1836, it was noted that prior to Wilkin's mastery of the Sanskrit language, "the language was not merely

---

1. J.C. Kapoor, *Bhagavad-gita: An International Bibliography of* 1785-1979 Imprints, (New York, Garland Publishing Company, 1983), p. xix.

unknown, but supposed to be unattainable by Europeans."[2] A letter to Wilkins from Sir William Jones, dated October 6, 1787, had this to say: "You are the first European who ever understood Sanskrit, and will, possibly, be the last."[3] Three years earlier, in 1784, Jones had written Wilkins that the "warriors of the M'hab'harat appear greater in my eyes than Agamemnon, Ajax, and Achilles appeared, when I read the Illiad."[4]

One of Wilkin's most memorable achievements was to take place, however, when he aided Sir William in organizing the Asiatick Society in Bengal. An enthusiastic and productive scholar, Wilkins helped Jones with this important Indological institution well after Jones had passed on. Wilkins, it is said, was an able scholar and consummate Indologist. But given the scarcity of information available to him at the time and the prejudices of his age, he was not without error in his interpretations.[5] The four defects mentioned in the beginning of this book come to mind.

At the same time, in America, a similar phenomenon was occurring in regard to Indological study. The American Oriental Society was founded in 1842, and some years later, with the evolution of Sanskrit research, Edward Elbridge Salisbury (1814-1901) was deemed the first American Orientalist of any repute. He taught at Yale (Elihu Yale was himself an Indophile and had a profound respect for Indian philosophy), influencing many others of high standing.

One of Salisbury's students at Yale, William Dwight Whitney (1827-1901), went on to become a greatly respected Sanskritist. In 1854, he became a senior professor of Sanskrit language and literature at Yale, wrote his classic *Sanksrit Grammer* (1879), and became an inspiration to all students of Indology.

Archeology In India

As this research was going on in Europe and America (but rarely in India), Alexander Cunningham (1814-1893) began a thirty-year expedition in the land that is renowned for the Sanskrit literature so

---

2 Ibid., p. xx.
3. Ibid.
4. Ibid.
5. Ibid., p. xxii.

admired by the Occidental Indologists. By studying India and her indigenous Vedic tradition, scholars were beginning to uncover a culture so alluring and fascinating that India was beginning to be seen as the superlative holy land. While this was pleasing to some, others, particularly Christian missionaries, balked at the prospect of having to acknowledge the sanctity of a tradition other than their own. Cunningham's expedition was commissioned by both the sincere Indophiles and by Christian missionaries. The archeological debates and conclusions that were instigated by Cunningham's research make up a considerable portion of this book.

From 1861 to 1866, the first Archeological Survey of India—which is often identified with the goals of Alexander Cunningham—was born. In its early days, it functioned intensively. But it suddenly ceased to exist.[6] The initial findings of the Archeological Survey were obscure, necessitating divergent explanations. Philosophical hermeneutics and complex polemics came into play. In addition to this confusion, there followed a few years of debate: Why should Western scholars bring to light the antiquity and profundity of Vedic culture? Perhaps European culture, and Christianity in particular, was more ancient and, indeed, more profound. Cunningham, for one, needed to know for sure.

By 1871, Cunningham returned to his post as director-general of the reformed Archeological Survey. Eighteen years later, however, the institution once again dissolved. This time due to the suggestion of James Burgess, Cunningham's successor, who plainly saw that much of the newly-discovered archeological and epigraphical evidence bore testimony to the antiquity of Vedic culture—to the pre-Christian worship of Lord Krishna. This was not the conclusion that Burgess had hoped he would find. Four years later, in 1902, the Archeological Survey was reformed once again—this time for good.

The results of the Survey's early work, especially the years in which Cunningham was presiding, are preserved in the volumes of *The Reports of the Archeological Survey of India*, the *New Imperial Series*, and the *Epigraphia Indica*. These are all used as references in this short work.

---

6. Maurizio Taddei, *India: Monuments of Civilization*, (New York, Grosset and Dunlap, 1978), p. 182.

Archeology And The Vaishnava Tradition

Ample archeological evidence exists for the antiquity of Vaishnavism, and most of this evidence is due to the work of the Archeological Survey. Even today, B.B. Lal, a top Indian archeologist, continues to uncover important finds. Director-general of the Archeological Survey from 1968 to 1972, Lal is still working diligently in his chosen field. In fact, he is currently directing an Indian national project: "Archeology of the Ramayana Sites." First conceived in 1977 by the Indian Institute for Advanced Study in Shimla and the Archeological Survey of India, the project calls for rigorous work, although it should see completion sometime later this year.[7] The goal of the project is to prove the historicity of the stories in the *Ramayana,* a Sanskrit text comprising over 14,000 verses. Great success has already been achieved.[8]

Such scholarly work can easily be appreciated by the intelligentsia of both Eastern and Western nations. But, once again, such work is also considered unnecessary from the perspective of the devotional tradition. After all, archeological evidence is, as mentioned in the beginning, imperfect at best. In fact, it requires a sort of devotional tradition of its own. A sort of beguiled faith. For its truths can never be consistently confirmed. Its adherents can never be certain.

Far be it from us, however, to minimize their faith. If faith is reasonable, and reposed in something worthwhile, then it serves a purpose and, indeed, enriches one's life. Further, it can even serve as a catalyst for deeper commitment, expressed in a more mature, developed kind of faith. It is said that St. Thomas, for instance, lacked faith in Jesus. He was thus known as "Doubting Thomas." But Jesus did not turn Thomas away. No. Rather, he gave Thomas evidence that he could understand. And so Thomas eventually became a believer. Thomas developed faith in Jesus through his faith in empirical evidence.

In a sense, this book can serve a similar purpose. Vedic culture actually speaks for itself. Anyone who is a practicing devotee of Lord Krishna, researching Vedic culture by taking part in it, has no

---

7. B.B. Lal, "A 2,000 Year-Old Feat of Hydraulic Engineering in India," *Archeology Magazine,* January/February, 1985, p.49.
8. Ibid.

problem with the antiquity of Krishna worship (Vaishnavism). Its primeval nature is obvious. Its pristine purity evident. Despite bogus accusations that Krishna worship is some "new cult" or "the work of the devil," in point of fact it is the most comprehensive and time-honored religious tradition known to man. This can be objectively proven and is documented in the books of His Divine Grace A.C. Bhaktivedanta Swami Prabhupada (as well as in the writings of prominent Indologists and historians the world over).

Now, as a humble offering at the lotus feet of my spiritual master and Godbrothers, I would like to submit that since so much work has been done in the field of Indology, presenting archeological, epigraphical, and numismatic evidence for the historicity and antiquity of Vaishnavism, I find it incumbent upon myself to use this evidence in the service of the Lord. If this evidence encourages even one person to take Vedic culture more seriously, then I will consider the publication of this book to have been successful.

MEGASTHENES

Compiled some 5,000 years ago, the Vedic literature is the world's chief source of information regarding the religion and culture of ancient India. Studied within the proper lineage of disciplic descent, the Vedas offer not only a storehouse of information for the sincere student of Indology, but a spiritual way of life that is both practical and profound.

Nonetheless, the literary work of Megasthenes (302-288 B.C.) has proven indispensable in regard to substantiating the pre-Christian roots of Krishna worship. In his writings, scholars find the earliest non-Vedic accounts of ancient Vaishnavism, her theology and culture. According to Megasthenes' view, the worship of Lord Krishna, the Supreme Personality of Godhead, was a central theme in India's devotional life. And he wrote on this subject extensively.

Unfortunately, none of Megasthenes' original writings have survived. But fragments of his work—and most certainly the essence—have been preserved through the medium of his early Greek and Latin commentators, such as Arrian, Diodorus, and Strabo.[9]

---

9. Benjamin Preciado-Solis, *The Krishna Cycle in the Puranas,* (Delhi, Motilal Banarsidass, 1984), p.21

These writers took great pains to salvage Megasthenes' *Indica*, which is today perhaps the most important work in the realm of Indological research.

Megasthenes journeyed from the Hellenistic world to India sometime in the third century B.C. He was an ambassador to the court of Chandragupta at Patliputra, where he was sent by the king of Taxila.[10] Little did our adventurous friend know that his preoccupation with pen and paper—notes on India and Indian religion—would be used in the twentieth century to finalize the debate between the comparative historicity and antiquity of Christianity and Krishna worship.

The Debate

It was with the British colonization of India and the development of Indology (largely by Christian missionaries) that a great debate over the relationship between Christianity and Krishna consciousness ensued. Perhaps the earliest claim that Christianity antedated Krishna worship, or Vaishnavism, was made by P. Georgi of Rome in 1762.[11] His claim was that the Sanskrit name Krishna, often pronounced *krishta*, could have easily been derived from the Greek name Christ. And yet he gave no reason why it could not be the other way around. Especially since Sanskrit, even then, was known to be much older than Greek. Today, it is rarely questioned: Krishna—His name and His religion—is unequivocally accepted as the older of the two. Exactly how this fact came to be discovered, however, recalls some of the most interesting pages in the literature of Indological study.

Georgi's theory was severely opposed by several important scholars, most significantly by Sir William Jones, who believed Krishna to be "one of the more ancient gods of India."[12] Jones, however, was also lacking in evidence. And so was Edward Moore, who convincingly asserted that the popular myths of the Greeks and other cultures had some basis in reality and were derived, ultimately,

---

10. Alan Dahlquist, *Megasthenes and Indian Religion*, (Delhi, Motilal Banarsidass, 1962), p.9.
11. P. Georgi, *Alphabetum Tibetanum*, (Rome, 1762), p.253.
12. J.W. McCrindle, *Ancient India as Described by Megasthenes and Arrian*, (Bombay, Thacker & Co., 1877), p.201.

from India. But this was all conjecture. Solid proof seemed scarce.

The Borrowing Theory

The debate soon gave rise to "the borrowing theory." Many scholars came to support this perspective, which asserted that the religion and culture of ancient India was not so ancient after all. In fact, according to the theory, Vedic ideology was simply "borrowed" from a ready and waiting Christianity.

The early proponents of this idea were many. Most of them, naturally, were Christians. Albrecht Weber, F. Lorinser, and Edward Washburn Hopkins were the most prominent scholars favoring Christianity as the older of the two religions.

Weber's monograph, *Uber die Krishna Janmashtami*, centered around the birth of Krishna. It brought to light many similarities involving the two divinities. Specifically, Weber pointed out that both Christ and Krishna's parents were involved in paying taxes at the time of the divine birth. He also made much of the fact that the activities of Kamsa and Herod, in the lives of Krishna and Jesus respectively, were almost identical. Finally, Weber was adamant about the connection between the divine names, Krishna and Christ. He went so far as to claim that the whole Vedic system of *avatar* ("divine incarnation") was "borrowed" from the conception of Christ's incarnation.

Lorinser added insult to injury with his comparative study of the *Bhagavad-gita* and the New Testament. He found great harmony between the two religious classics. But he insisted that the original, of course, was the New Testament, and the *Bhagavad-gita* was simply an expurgated derivative.[13]

And then there was the work of Edward W. Hopkins, noted for his essay entitled *Christ in India*. His comparative study of the *Gita* and the Gospel of John was considered brilliant and was noted by contemporaries around the world. Hopkins' version of "the borrowing theory," moreover, engendered a slight variation on the others. He contended that although Krishna worship was perhaps earlier, the personality originally worshipped became an entirely new god—just as Christianity arrived in India. In other words, Krishna was

---

13. Dahlquist, op. cit., p.13.

merely some "tribal god" who achieved "Supreme Godhood" when His followers were influenced by Christian thought.[14]

Thus Hopkins believed that Christianity exerted a marked influence on the characteristics of Krishna due to the preaching of St. Thomas, one of the original twelve Apostles. Exactly how this is supposed to have taken place is unknown. All that is certain about St. Thomas' stay in India is that his following was small and that he was eventually martyred.[15]

As the supporters of "the borrowing theory" came forward with new arguments for the originality of Christianity, their new opposition grew stronger, often using the very facts and figures that were uncovered by the opposing side. Each would interpret the data in their own way. The similarity between the names—Krishna and Christ—became a focal point in such debates. But despite decades of two-way arguments, it was eventually determined that the name Christ was taken from the Greek *Christos*, which is derived from the Sanskrit *Krishta*, or Krishna.[16] Just the opposite of what Georgi taught.

Megasthenes

The roof started to cave in as scholars from within the Christian tradition, such as Auguste Barth, began to challenge Weber, claiming that the ancient, respectable tradition of Krishna worship antedated Christianity.[17] "At least," Barth had written, "both religions existed simultaneously and each had evolved independent of the other."[18]

Dr. R.G. Bhandarkar, a scholar of Indian origin, discovered convincing evidence that Vaishnavism existed before the Christian Era. The allusions to Krishna in Patanjali's *Mahabhasya* went undisputed among proponents of the borrowing theory. However, this work was undeniably composed before the Christian Era, thus establishing the pre-Christian roots of Krishna worship.

If this evidence went largely unnoticed, Bhandarkar further pointed to a passage in the *Panini Sutra* (4.3.98), where the word *vasudevar*

---

14. Ibid.
15. A. Faber-Kaiser, *Jesus Died in Kashmir*, (England, Gordon & Cremonesi, 1976), p.81
16. Dahlquist, op. cit., pp.15-16.
17. Auguste Barth, *Les Religions de l'Inde*, (Paris, 1914), p.132.
18. Ibid.

junabhyam-vun is mentioned. Here, Vasudeva (Krishna) is worshipped in connection with Arjuna, His devotee. According to Bhandarkar, this verse would place Krishna worship in at least the fifth century B.C.[19] Still, there were arguments pro and con. Much was left unsettled.

Finally, Dr. Christian Lassen was the first to bring Megasthenes into the discussion.[20] In his book, *Indische Altertumskunde,* Lassen refers to Megasthenes' *Indica,* wherein "Krishna" is clearly described under the pseudonym Heracles. Both the River Yamuna and the town of Mathura are mentioned, and this "Heracles" is seen as the Supreme Lord, worshipped by the residents of Mathura.[21] Scholarly research has since conclusively established that the name "Heracles" was derived from the Sanskrit Hari-kul-eesh (i.e., "a manifestation of the Supreme Controller, Hari [Krishna]").

Since Megasthenes was known to have lived during the third century before Christ, the borrowing theory suffered a tremendous setback. Even the most fundamentalist of the Christian missionaries were now forced to ask themselves: Who was borrowing from whom? In scholarly circles, the antiquity of Krishna worship was quickly becoming accepted, especially among well-informed Indologists and Sanskritists.

One prominent Indologist, Richard Garbe, was even more outspoken than Lassen, and claimed that the testimony of Megasthenes was incontestable.[22] Garbe's analysis of the situation was so convincing and eloquent that Alan Dahlquist, who is generally aligned with proponents of the borrowing theory, was virtually forced to admit that Garbe "exploded Weber's theory once and for all."[23]

At the beginning of the twentieth century the subject was laid to rest by John M. Robertson, researcher extraordinaire, who wrote, "Krishna is proved by documentary evidence to have flourished in India before the Christian Era."[24] After a lifetime of study, the same scholar reported, "....It is settled that the most conservative Sanskrit scholarship on the continent not only admits but insists on the pre-

19. R.G. Bhandarkar, *Allusions to Krishna in Patanjali's Mahabbasya,* (I.A., III: 1874), p.14.
20. Dahlquist, op. cit., p.20.
21. David R. Godine, *Krishna: The Divine Lover,* (London, CHP Editions, 1982), p.105.
22. Richard Garbe, *Indiem und das Christum,* (Tubingen: 1914), p.73
23. Dahlquist, op. cit., p.18.
24. John M. Robertson, *Christianity and Mythology,* (London, Watts & Co., 1910), p.273.

Christian character of Krishna."[25]

This, along with the other archeological evidences subsequently discovered (and recorded in this book), have led a good number of scholars to support Lassen in his conclusions, to the extent that the official statement on the subject was recorded for all time in *The Cambridge History of India*: Krishna worship predates Christianity.[26]

Of course, from the spiritual perspective, Krishna and Christ are both eternal personalities. Thus there is no question of which came first, and any attempt to categorize them in this way may be considered a priori absurd. Theologically, Krishna is the father, as is stated in the *Bhagavad-gita*, and Christ is the son, according to the New Testament. Both the Supreme Lord and His son are completely transcendental, and they exist beyond time. It is said, in fact, that in the spiritual realm, time is conspicuous by its absence. As far as their manifest pastimes in the material world, however, Krishna is considered to have come first, appearing some 5,000 years ago. Christ, as we know, appeared only 2,000 years ago.

Conclusion

This archeological survey does not subscribe to spiritual dogma per se, and so we must proceed according to the parameters of our chosen discipline. Megasthenes is accepted by all Indologists as the most important literary evidence in regard to the antiquity of Krishna worship. Megasthenes establishes the God of Mathura from at least the third century B.C.—and this is considered important because it allows Krishna worship to stand alone, uninfluenced by Christianity, which came later. Certainly the name Krishna came first, and this has been documented conclusively by the scholars who have studied Megasthenes.

But more important than the writings of Megasthenes is the Vedic literature. According to *Shrimad Bhagavatam*, Lord Krishna appeared on earth 5,000 years ago, and He was worshipped as the Supreme Personality of Godhead from the very beginning of His appearance. This knowledge has been passed down in an unbroken preceptorial succession.

---

25. Ibid., pp.158-59.
26. *The Cambridge History Of India*, Vol. 1-6, (Cambridge, 1922-32) Suppl. Vol., Cambridge 1953, p.167.

This succession embodies a "borrowing" process of its own. Vedic knowledge is originally enunciated by the Lord to the first created being, who is known as Brahma. Next, Narada Muni, a celebrated sage, "borrowed" the information and delivered it intact to Shrila Vyasadev. In this way, Vedic knowledge is carefully passed down, person to person, and today it has been preserved in the books of His Divine Grace Swami Prabhupada. The reader is advised to "borrow" this knowledge as well. And then to pass it on to everyone he meets.

THE HELIODORUS COLUMN

Heliodorus was a Greek ambassador to India in the second century B.C. Few details are known about the diplomatic relations between the Greeks and the Indians in those days, and, unfortunately, still less is known about Heliodorus. Nevertheless the column he erected at Besnagar in central India about 113 B.C.[27] is considered one of the most important archeological finds on the Indian subcontinent. The column's inscription has remarkable historical value—for the Krishna consciousness movement and for the world—because it stands as irrefutable evidence that the philosophy of Krishna consciousness had made an impact on Western minds at least twenty-two hundred years ago.

Heliodorus was sent to the court of King Bhagabhadra by Antialkidas, the Greek king of Taxila. The kingdom of Taxila was part of the Bactrian region in northwest India, which was conquered by Alexander the Great in 325 B.C. By the time of Antialkidas, the area under Greek rule included what is today Afghanistan, Pakistan, and Punjab.[28]

The column erected by Heliodorus first came to the attention of Western eyes in 1877, during an archeological survey by General Alexander Cunningham. The inscription, however, went unnoticed, because of the pillar's thick coating of red lead. It had been the custom of pilgrims who had worshipped there to smear the column with

---

27. Survita Jaiswal, *The Origin and Development of Vaishnavism,* (New Delhi, Munshiram Manoharlal, 1980), p.116.
28. A.L. Basham, *A Cultural History of India,* (London, Clearendon Press, 1974), p.431.

vermilion paint. Deducing the time frame of the column from its shape, Cunningham determined that it was from the period of the Imperial Guptas[29] (A.D. 300-550)· Thirty-two years later, however, when the inscription was finally brought to light, it became clear that the monument was several centuries older.[30]

In January 1901, a Mr. Lake discerned what he thought was some lettering on the lower part of the column, and the removal of some paint proved him right. Dr. J.H. Marshall, who accompanied Mr. Lake, described the discovery in the *Journal of the Royal Asiatic Society* in 1909. Cunningham, Marshall explained, had been mistaken about the age of the column and "could little have dreamt of the value of the record which he just missed discovering....A glance at the few letters exposed was all that was needed to show that the column was many centuries earlier than the Gupta era. This was, indeed, a surprise to me, but a far greater one was in store when the opening lines of the inscription came to be read."[31]

A reproduction of the inscription, along with the translation of the ancient Brahmi text, is given here as it appeared in the *Journal of the Royal Asiatic Society*:

1) *Devadevasa Va[sude]vasa Garudadhvajo ayam*
2) *karito i[a] Heliodorena bhaga-*
3) *vatena Diyasa putrena Takhasilakena*
4) *Yonadatena agatena maharajasa*
5) *Amtalikitasa upa[m]ta samkasam-rano*
6) *Kasiput[r]asa [Bh]agabhadrasa tratarasa*
7) *vasena [chatu]dasena rajena vadhamanasa*

"This Garuda-column of Vasudeva (Vishnu), the God of gods, was erected here by Heliodorus, a worshipper of Vishnu and the son of Dion. Heliodorus was an inhabitant of Taxila, who came as a Greek ambassador from the Great King Antialkidas to King Kasiputra Bhagabhadra, the Savior, then reigning prosperously in the fourteenth year of his kingship."

---

29. *Journal of the Asiatic Society*, (London, JRAS, 1909), pp.1053-54.
30. Ibid.
31. Ibid.

1) *Trini amutapadani—[su] anuthitani*
2) *nayamti svaga damo chago apramado*

"Three immortal precepts (footsteps)... when practiced lead to heaven—self-restraint, charity, conscientiousness."

From the inscription it is clear that Heliodorus was a Vaishnava, a devotee of Vishnu. Vasudeva and Vishnu are both popular names of Krishna—the Supreme Personality of Godhead, and Heliodorus's endorsement of self-restraint *(damo)*, self-sacrifice *(chago)*, and alertness *(apramado)* further corroborates his status as a devotee of Krishna. Professor Kunja Govinda Goswami of Calcutta University concludes that Heliodorus "was well acquainted with the texts dealing with the Bhagavat [Vaishnava] religion."[32]

To our knowledge, Heliodorus is the earliest Westerner on record to convert to Vaishnavism. But some scholars, most notably A.L. Basham[33] and Thomas Hopkins, are of the opinion that Heliodorus was not the only Greek convert to Vaishnavism. Hopkins, chairman of the department of religious studies at Franklin and Marshall College, has said, "Heliodorus was presumably not the only foreigner who was converted to Vaishnava devotional practices—although he might have been the only one to erect a column, at least one that is still extant. Certainly there must have been many others."[34]

It is interesting to note that the column has other historical merits. Around the turn of the century, a number of Indologists (Weber, Macnicol, and others) had noted "points of similarity" between the Vaishnava philosophy of unalloyed devotion to Krishna and Christian doctrine. They argued that devotion to Krishna must have been a perverted offshoot of Christianity, and cited similarity between stories about Krishna and Christ to further support their claim.[35] But the discovery of the inscription on the Heliodorus column laid their

32. Kunja Govinda Goswami, *A Study of Vaishnavism*, (Calcutta, Oriental Book Agency, 1956), p.6.
33. A.L. Basham, *The Wonder That Was India*, third edition, (Oxford, Taplinger Publishing Co., 1967), p.60
34. Steven J. Gelberg, ed., *Hare Krishna, Hare Krishna*, (New York, Grove Press, 1983), p.117.
35. M.D. Khare, "Comments on the Heliodorus Pillar at Besnagar," in *Puratattva*, (No.8, 1965, p.178.

speculations to rest. Here was conclusive archeological proof that the Vaishnava tradition antedated Christianity by at least two hundred years.

The column also struck down another erroneous notion. For centuries it was the common belief that India's orthodox tradition did not accept converts. An Islamic historian, Abu Raihan Alberuni, who went to India in A.D. 1017, tried to explain in his book *Indica* why the Indian orthodoxy did not admit foreigners. Alberuni suggested that the practice developed only after the Moslem incursion into India sometime after A.D. 674.[36] Antagonism between Moslems and Hindus seems to be the main reason behind the non-conversion practice. For many centuries prior to the Moslem presence, however, there had been no bar to conversion into the orthodox fold, as attested by the Heliodorus column.

Vaishnavism is the path being followed by the members of the International Society for Krishna Consciousness. Western converts are impressed, just as Heliodorus must have been, by the philosophy and practice of Vaishnavism. Ironically, however, misinformed persons try to defame the Krishna consciousness movement and the time-tested tradition that it represents. They try to lump in the members of ISKCON with the faddish cults of the day, many of which are known to have questionable practices and motives.

In the face of the historical precedent set by Heliodorus, these accusations leveled against the modern Vaishnavas are clearly unwarranted. The Heliodorus column, erected in honor of Lord Shri Krishna, is proof that the Vaishnava philosophy of devotion to Lord Krishna was winning followers from the West long before its recent inception as the International Society for Krishna Consciousness.

THE MORA WELL INSCRIPTION

About seven miles west of Lord Krishna's birthplace, Mathura, stands a small village named Mora. This ancient dwelling place for sages remains an unimposing relic, a humble smattering of the past with a message for today. That message, embodied in the Mora Well

---

36. Ahmad H. Dani. *Alberuni's India,* (Lexhore, India, University of Islamabad, 1973), p.37.

Stone Slab Inscription (First Century B.C.), is that Krishna was lovingly worshipped before the Christian Era—and not alone, but with His associates.[37]

According to the inscription, "the five heroes of the Vrishni clan" were considered divine, and these "heroes" have been identified by thorough scholarly research: Krishna, Balarama [Vasudeva and Sankarshan], Pradyumna, Samba, and Anirudha.[38] The credit for the discovery goes, once again, to Alexander Cunningham.

In 1882, only five years after he discovered the Heliodorus Column, Cunningham came upon a large inscribed slab that formed part of the terrace of an ancient wall (the Mora Well inscription). Soon a transcript and facsimile of the inscription were published in the *Archeologial Survey of India's Annual Report.*[39] At that time, the inscription was already incomplete, more than half of it having peeled away on the right side. And since then it has become much more seriously damaged. Although the most important parts can still be read.

Attempted Forgery

Several decades after Cunningham initially discovered it, the valuable stone slab was moved to the Mathura Museum by a fledging archeologist named Dr. Vogel, who worked under the supervision of renowned scholar Pandit Radha Krishna.[40] It has since been brought to light that Vogel had attempted to edit the Mora Well inscription at that time.[41] However, the original contents of the inscription were by then (1909) too well known in scholarly circles. It was already recorded for posterity.

The attempt to edit the inscription is instructive. Many early archeologists in India were Christian—and they made no bones about their motivation. In the early 1800s, for instance, some of the greatest progress in the field of Sanskrit and Indological study was made at

---

37. J.N. Banerjee, *The Development of Hindu Iconography*, (Calcutta, Calcutta University Press, 1956), p.94.
38. *Vayu Purana*, 97: 1-4., Also see J.N. Banerjee, *Pauranic and Tantric Religion*, (Calcutta, Calcutta University Press, 1966), pp.29-31.
39. *Archeological Survey of India's Annual Report*, (Vol. XX, 1885), p.49.
40. *Epigraphia Indica*, (Delhi, Vol. XXIV, 1937-38), p.194.
41. Ibid.

Oxford University. H.H. Wilson became the first Boden Professor of Sanskrit at that particular school. His successor, the famous professor M. Monier-Williams, has clearly delineated the originial purpose and motivation for Indological study: "I must draw attention to the fact that I am only the second occupant of the Boden Chair, and that its founder, Colonel Boden, stated most explicitly in his will (dated August 15, 1811) that the special object of his munificent bequest was to promote the translation of scriptures from Sanskrit—so as to enable his countrymen to proceed in the conversion of the natives of India to the Christian religion."[42]

In eighteenth-century Europe, religion meant Christianity—plain and simple. One was irreligious if one was not a Christian. And one was illiterate if one could not read the English Bible. Nevermind the exalted Vedic texts—hundreds of volumes in length—written in the highly sophisticated Sanskrit language (Indeed, *Sanskrit* means "highly evolved" or "polished"!). To those who actually made an in-depth and unbiased comparative study, it gradually became clear that racism and religious prejudice were the sole motivating factors behind the enthusiastic and "munificent" attempts of the early Indologists. One Indian historian summed up these ideas in the following way: "This attitude of Europeans toward Indians was due to a sense of racial superiority—a cherished conviction which was shared by every Englishman in India, from the highest to the lowest."[43]

Racial Prejudice

Alexander Duff (1806-1878) soon founded Scots College, in Calcutta, which he envisioned as a "headquarters for a great campaign against Hinduism."[44] Duff's avowed mission was to convert "the natives" by enrolling them, often times freely, in English-run schools and colleges; at these schools he placed emphasis on learning the English language, "inadvertantly" teaching Christianity through the medium of literacy. Inevitably, in learning English, the

---

42. Sir M. Monier-Williams, *Sanskrit English Dictionary*, (preface, 1899), p.IX.
43. R.C. Majumdar, et al., ed., *History and Culture of the Indian People*, (Bombay, Bharatya Vidya Bhavan, 1965), Vol. 10, p.348.
44. George Smith, *Dictionary of National Biography*, (Oxford University Press, 1950), Vol. 6, p.126.

Indian people were virtually forced to learn the Bible, even though they were initially quite satisfied with their own religion. The Indian people were deliberately taught that Christianity was the superior form of spirituality, and that their own religious heritage was backward and uncivilized.[45]

This state of affairs was precipitated, of course, by the Battle of Plassey, in 1757, when the Indian army was defeated by the British East India Company. As history relates, the British gained full control of India just after this historic battle. And they immediately began to impose their beliefs upon the Indian people. Some background information on this phenomenon has been given in Satsvarupa Das Goswami's *Readings in Vedic Literature* (in the chapter called "The First Indologists").

Dr. Vogel, in attempting to distort the Mora Well inscription, was right in line with many of his predecessors in the world of Indology and archeology. Nonetheless, Cunningham's work, published in an authoritative scholarly journal, was done prior to Vogel's attempt, and he clearly established the supremacy of Krishna, Balaram, and the other three Vrishnis.[46] The Mora Well inscription, dating from before the time of Christ, is thus an indispensable addition to the purpose of this book, and scholars around the world agree on the importance and significance of the discovery.

DVARAKA: KRISHNA'S MAJESTIC ABODE

The apparent remains of ancient Dvaraka, the city in which Lord Krishna reigned as king some 5,000 years ago, were recently discovered by a team of archeologists exploring the Arabian Sea off the coast of present-day Dvaraka (in the Jamnagar district of Gujarat).

According to the Vedic scriptures, Lord Krishna lived there as a king with large palaces, retinue, and chivalrous pastimes of royal glory. So magnificent are the accounts of His activities in Dvaraka, that prior to the recent discoveries many refused to believe that Lord Krishna really displayed His divinely majestic abode on this earth (It

---

45. H.G. Rawlinson, *The British Achievement in India*, (London, Hodge Pub., 1948), p.53.
46. *Epigraphia India*, (Delhi, Vol. XXIV, 1937-38), p.194.

has an eternal counterpart in the kingdom of God).

Expert divers have discovered ruins and large building blocks for ancient temple structures deeply embedded underwater at the entry point of the long-standing harbor at mainland Dvaraka. Structures of the submerged land of Krishna and lustrous redware pottery were also found in the area.

Official Conclusions

Archeologists have concluded that these artifacts date from the time of the Harappan civilization, which came to a mysterious end at about B.C. 3000, corresponding with the last days of Krishna's manifest pastimes. These and other recent evidences suggest that the ancient kingdom, Dvaraka, was inundated by the Arabian Sea between B.C. 1500 and 1400. Many scholars, however, believe the relics are much older. Some even say that the submerging of Dvaraka may be the historical act upon which the Atlantis legends are built. And the Vedic tradition, again, says that Krishna's kingdom flourished no less than 5,000 years ago.

The diving expedition used sophisticated underwater vaccuum tubes and side-scan sonar to locate the Dvaraka site. "This project is helping us to learn about our history, our culture, and our religion," said V.V. Varadachari, the director of India's National Institute of Oceanography.

The expedition on Dvaraka, carried out by S.R. Rao of India's same Institute, is part of a three-year program for exploring the submerged parts of Dvaraka and Kaveripoompatnam, and for retrieving at least one historically significant shipwreck in Indian waters. The findings, however, continue to vastly exceed the explorers' expectations.

Thus far five cities have been identified in this area, each traceable to the time of Krishna. The latest findings are believed to be the central core of Krishna's main city, which was originally constructed by the demigod Vishvakarma on an island covering a space of 96 square miles. Upon Krishna's disappearance, say the traditional texts, the island was engulfed by the ocean.

On shore, archeologists have unearthed an entire temple-like structure beneath the present-day Dvaraka temple, which is itself 2,000 years old and includes a chamber said to date back to the time of Krishna. Other findings include sculpted pillars and carved figurines of celestial beings similar to decorations within the present temple. Research continues to bear fruit.

THE GHOSUNDI INSCRIPTION

In addition to the Heliodorus column and the Mora Well, there is another, similar find of equal importance. The Ghosundi inscription has been praised by Indologists and archeologists as conclusive evidence in determining the antiquity of Krishna worship.

First brought to the attention of scholars by Kaviraja Shyamala Dasa in *The Journal of the Bengal Asiatic Society*,[47] the Ghosundi inscription is now located in the Victoria Hall museum at Udaipur and was discovered at the village of Ghosundi, in the Chitor District of Rajasthan.[48] The inscription is almost identical to that of Hathi-vada, which was found nearby. Both inscriptions are invaluable to scholars who seek to establish the pre-Christian roots of Krishna worship.

The composed text of both the Ghosundi and Hathi-vada inscriptions is only partially revealed, and it has been translated as follows:

"[This] stone enclosure, called the Narayana Vataka, for the worship of bhagavan Shankarshan and bhagavan Vasudeva, the invincible Lords of all, [was erected] by the [Bhaga]vata king of the line of Gaja, Sarvatata the victorious, who performed an ashvamedha sacrifice..."[49]

The original characters of the inscription are in northern Brahmi script, which is a form of Sanskrit from the later Maurya or early Sunga period (corresponding to the second century before Christ).

Interpretation

Scholars believe that the stone enclosure referred to in the text

---

47. Kaviraja Shyamala Dasa, *The Journal of the Bengal Asiatic Society*, (Bengal: Vol. LVI, part I, p.77ff., No. 1 and pl. V).
48. *Epigraphia Indica*, (Calcutta: Government of India Press, 1921-22), Vol. XVII, pp.26-27.
49. Ibid.

was a temple dedicated to the worship of Shankarshan (Balaram) and Vasudeva (Krishna), who are described as "the invincible Lords of all." Thus, the inscription carries much the same message as the Mora Well: Krishna and Balaram were worshiped together well before the time of Christ.

Alternative View

There is another view of "the stone enclosure" that is particularly interesting and relevant to out treatment of the subject. Indian academician J.C. Ghosh contends that the interpretation of the Sanskrit word *pujashilaprakar* should not be "the stone enclosure [shilaprakar] for worship [puja]," as is commonly understood.[50] Rather, he saw it as "a rampart for the stone object of worship." Ghosh further contends that the "stone object" was clearly Shalagram Shila, a type of stone that is to this day worshiped as Vishnu, or Krishna.[51] Whether one accepts the view that the "stone object" refers to the remains of a temple or to the sacred Shalagram Shila, the Ghosundi inscription supports the premise of this book.

Shrimad Bhagavatam

Archeological evidence aside, tradition teaches that Krishna and Balaram were worshiped long before this period. And the *Bhagavat-purana*, also known as the *Shrimad Bhagavatam*, gives elaborate details about Their transcendental activities some fifty centuries ago. These activities were glorified and worshipped even as they were enacted.

According to the *Bhagavatam* (1:1:20), "Lord Shri Krishna, the Personality of Godhead, along with Balaram, played like a human being, and so masked He performed many superhuman acts." His Divine Grace Shrila Prabhupada comments, "The specific mention of the word Bhagavan in this text indicates that Balaram and Krishna are the original forms of the Lord....Krishna is the Supreme Personality of Godhead, and Balaram is the first plenary manifestation of the Lord. From Balaram comes the first phalanx of plenary expansions, Vasudeva,

---

50. J.N. Banerjee, *Development of Hindu Iconography*, (Calcutta, University of Calcutta Press, 1941), p.101.
51. J.C. Gosh, "Notes on the Ghosundi Inscription" in *The Indian Historical Quarterly*, (India: 1933), Vol. 9, p.799.

Samkarshan, Aniruddha and Pradyumna. Lord Shri Krishna is Vasudeva, and Balaram is Samkarshan."

While the Vedic idea of Shankarshan is quite complex, it is evident that Krishna and Balaram were understood to at least be manifestations of God even in the puranic period. A deeper study of the tradition reveals them to be alternate features of the original Personality of Godhead.

But the Ghosundi Inscription tells us something more about Krishna/Balaram worship. It tells us something about the caliber of devotee who worshipped Them. Many scholars assumed that since Krishna, in His earthly pastimes, played the role of a kshatriya king, He was worshipped only by the kshatriya class. The same scholars that make this claim also support the theory that Krishna was a "pious king from Mathura" who became celebrated in legend after his death and later became elevated to the position of a deva, or god. Both notions, however, have been proven erroneous.

According to K.P. Jayaswal, of the Archeological Survey of India, the inscription at Ghosundi shows that the followers of Krishna included brahmins, the priestly or intellectual class.[52] Research in this area has laid all debate to rest.

And as far as whether or not Krishna was some "pious king" who was later deified, there are endless puranic quotes that establish the fact that He was known as the Lord in His own time. All of the great sages proclaim this of Him. Devala, Vyasa, Asita, Narada, Brahma—they attest to Lord Krishna's Lordship unequivocally. Even Arjuna, the hero of *Bhagavad-gita*, India's unexcelled treatise on metaphysics, declares Krishna to be "Lord of lords; God of gods; the source of all spiritual and material worlds." The tradition speaks for itself.

AFTERWORD

The evidences discussed in this book point squarely to the pre-Christian roots of Krishna worship. This restricts our subject to Vaishnavism. If we were to bring in earlier "Vedic" evidence, we could convincingly show an ancient culture based on unified non-sectarian religious principles. But that is not our goal. And so we have confined

---

52. *Epigraphia Indica*, Op. cit.

our treatment of the subject specifically to Krishna worship, or Vaishnavism.

There are other evidences for the antiquity of Krishna worship as well—archeological, epigraphical, numismatic. The Nanaghat Inscription, for instance, is another tribute to the dual worship of Krishna and Balaram.[53] From the Deccan, in the modern state of Maharashtra, the Nanaghat Inscription of Queen Naganika in the Nanaghat cave, Thana District, mentions the names of Vasudeva and Shankarshan, and equates Them with the Supreme Lord.[54] This inscription has been conclusively proven, on epigraphical grounds, to come from the second half of the first century before Christ.[55]

The *Artha-shastra* of Kautilya (Chanakya Pandit), generally accepted as originating in the fourth century B.C., reveals a *mantra* which can force animals to sleep. One of the introductory lines of this *mantra* mentions Krishna and Kamsa (the Lord's avowed enemy) and refers to the Vrishni Dynasty into which Krishna appeared.[56] All scholars familiar with these statements from the *Arthashastra* attest to their antiquity.

And then there are the grammatical works. Panini and Patanjali were already mentioned. But even before Panini, in *Nirukta*, Yaska's brilliant etymological work ascribed to the fifth century B.C.,[57] there is mention of an incident that presupposes the existence of Krishna. All of the elements of the stealing of the Shyamantaka Jewel are described, along with a description of two of Krishna's wives, Jambavati and Satyabhama.[58]

In the *Baudhayana Dharma Sutra*, attributed to the fourth century B.C.,[59] there exists an invocation to Vishnu wherein He is respectfully called by twelve different names, and among them are three popular names for Krishna: Keshava, Govinda, and Damodar.

53. D.C. Sircar, *Select Inscriptions Bearing on Indian History and Civilizations*, (Calcutta, University of Calcutta Press, 1965), second edition, Vol. I, p.192.
54. Ibid.
55. Ibid.
56. R.P. Kangle, *The Kautilya Arthashastra*, (India, University of Bombay, 1963), part II, pp.13-14.
57. M.A. Mehendale, "Nirukta Notes IV: Yaska's Etymology of Danda," *Journal of the American Oriental Society*, (1960), Vol. 80, pp.112-15.
58. Ibid.
59. G. Buhler, *The Sacred Laws of the Aryas*, (The Sacred Books of the East series), Vol. 14, 1882, p.254.

Further evidence for the antiquity of Vaishnavism can be gleaned from the writings of travellers. Megasthenes has already been mentioned, but the serious reader may research Quintus Curtius and Ptolemy who have both written extensively on the subject.[60]

The numismatic evidence is just as compelling. The coins of the Kushana kings attest to the antiquity of Krishna worship. Excavations at Ai-Khanum, along the border of the Soviet Union with Afghanistan, conducted by Dr. P. Bernard of a French archeological delegation, brought to light six rectangular bronze coins issued by the Indo-Greek ruler Agathocles (about 180-165 B.C.).[61] These coins, with copy in both Greek and Brahmi scripts, show Vishnu, or Vasudeva, carrying a chakra and a pear-shaped "vase" (or conchshell) on the reverse.[62] Such numismatic evidence is not uncommon.

Nonetheless, there are many who will maintain that the Krishna religion is new, a cult, despite all evidence to the contrary. This view is obviously ill-founded, although it may hold merit for those who find it convenient, for those who find the truth too jarring. Still, if Vaishnavism is to be considered a new cult, then Christianity must be considered so as well, for as we have seen, Krishna worship predates the Christian religion. Moreover, Vedic texts indicate that the Krishna religion is the original form of religious truth, and a sincere soul, before debating the veracity of this statement, would have to at least make a thorough investigation of it. Indeed, if it *is* true, then one must research the Vedic tradition, for one can learn a great deal about one's own religion by studying its source. There are no bones about it.

60. Enrico, Isacco, ed., *Krishna, The Divine Lover*, (London, Serindia Pub., David R. Godine, 1982), p.137.

61. A.K. Narain, "Two Hindu Divinities on the Coins of Agathocles from Ai-Khanum," *The Journal of the Numismatic Society of India*, (1973), Vol. XXXV, pp.73-77.

62. Ibid.

2

DID JESUS GO TO INDIA?

What did Jesus Christ do from the time he was twelve to the age of thirty? We are aware of his miraculous birth. The Bible also records the famous temple incident at age twelve. Then we are reintroduced to him at age thirty, being baptized at the River Jordan. With all due respect for his accomplishments after that—we are left with eighteen years unaccounted for.

Unimportant? Quite the contrary! If we are to accept that Jesus Christ changed the face of the earth in a three-year ministry—and he did—then eighteen missing years becomes vitally important. In the life of a person who is considered God incarnate by many—and at least a great saint by others—every moment is valuable. Every gesture is instructive. Every pastime is precious.

But the Bible is silent about the missing years. Since 1947 a veritable storehouse of scrolls and fragments have been discovered at the Dead Sea in Israel and at Nag Hammadi in Egypt. While these discoveries did shed some new light on first century Palestine and biblical culture in general, they had very little to say about "the lost years of Jesus," as the eighteen years have come to be called.

Still, the newly discovered manuscripts served to illuminate our understanding of innovation and interpolation in Western religious literature, especially in regard to noncanonical works known as the *Apocrypha* and the *Pseudepigrapha.* These were officially considered heretical by the Roman Catholic Church but were originally part of the Christian literary tradition. Through the Dead Sea and Nag Hammadi finds, scholars became aware that organized Christendom was highly selective in its promulgation of transcendental truth. There was much the Church was keeping from us—and we wanted to know all the details.

Thus, many began to reconsider the eighteen missing years of Jesus. Books by theologians, religionists and independent researchers inundated the market. Reverend C.R. Potter, for instance, released an informative book in 1962, *The Lost Years of Jesus Revealed.* Scholars Anne Read and J. Furst informed the world of Edgar Cayce's work in this area by each publishing their own fascinating book on the subject. In 1976, Andreas Faber-Kaiser contributed his exceptional work, *Jesus Died in Kashmir,* which not only thoroughly explained what happened during the eighteen missing years but also postulated a convincing and revolutionary theory of what transpired after the crucifixion, when Jesus was taken down from the cross (we will return to this "Kashmir hypothesis" later).

And perhaps the most recent work on Jesus' eighteen missing years is by Elizabeth Clare Prophet, whose comprehensive book, *The Lost Years of Jesus,* deals with every nuance of the subject. It should be noted, furthermore, that all of the above researchers—among others whom we shall soon mention—have found (to their satisfaction!) that Jesus did indeed travel to India. Reverend Potter, however, was more inclined to believe that Jesus' eighteen missing years were spent among the Essenes. Nonetheless, even the Reverend is ready to admit that the time may have been divided between studying with the Essenes and a journey to India.

The most famous contemporary work about Jesus' travels, however, comes from a husband-and-wife team, Dick and Janet Bock, whose painstaking research bore fruit in a film, *The Lost Years* (1978), and a book, *The Jesus Mystery* (1980). Says author and filmmaker Janet Bock: "It gradually dawned on us that those years were missing because someone had taken them out of the records, out of the Bible.

We could not imagine Jesus would have suddenly appeared in Galilee at the age of 30 and hidden the major part of his life from the disciples he loved and asked to follow him. And it really doesn't seem possible those years were so unimportant as to be dismissed without a word...So the idea grew that at some point what had been known about those years in his life had been deleted. In examining historical records of the early Christian Church, it became evident that early Church councils, especially the First Council of Nicea in 325 A.D., changed many points of doctrine....Those missing years were expunged because they did not coincide with the political needs of a growing Church."

Research in the last forty years—by the Bocks and the others mentioned above—unveiled a controversy obscured since the latter part of the last century and the early part of this one. This controversy—about Jesus' travels in India—began in 1894, when a Russian journalist, Nicolai Notovitch, published a mysterious and provocative book entitled *The Unknown Life of Jesus Christ.*

Just after the Turko-Russian War, it seems, Notovitch began a journey to the Orient. By 1887 he arrived in Kashmir, where he had heard of a Buddhist convent in Leh, the capital of Ladakh. Out of curiosity and perhaps providence he decided to visit the monks of Leh. There he was told of an ancient document. The lama in charge was quite secretive—but he did reveal that the document was about the life of Saint Issa. (The Latin spelling of Jesus is Iesus; in Arabic, it is Isa. It should be mentioned, moreover, that Isa is the Sanskrit root for the word Isvara, an Indian name for God literally meaning "the Supreme Controller.")

Notovitch was told that the ancient Pali manuscripts were to be found in the palace of the Dalai Lama, and these ancient works were even copies of older Sanskrit versions. Copies of these copies existed in several Buddhist monasteries along the countryside. Notovitch realized that he was fortunate enough to be at one of these monasteries.

The desire to see these scrolls was now becoming an obsession, and Notovitch offered the head lama three gifts—an alarm clock, a watch, and a thermometer—hoping the Buddhist priest would be so kind as to show him the life of Saint Issa in return. No luck.

As he was leaving the monastery on his horse, however, Notovitch hurt his leg and was forced to return, much to his good fortune. At his bedside the chief lama, now taking care of him, finally unveiled two big volumes in cardboard covers. This, the lama thought, would make the weary Russian traveller happy. Indeed it did. Here, written on decaying leaves, was the story of Saint Issa.

Notovitch's leg quickly healed. But not before he could secure an interpreter for the Issa manuscript. Noting down the story word-for-word, Notovitch soon returned to the West and published *The Unknown Life of Jesus Christ*.

The book informs us that at age thirteen Jesus left the home of Mary and Joseph in Nazareth. He travelled with a merchant caravan to the holy cities of India and even to the sacred Ganges River. Later, he left for Egypt to penetrate the mysteries of the Great Pyramid. And heading back, he explored the diverse philosophies of Athens and Persepolis. He returned to Israel when he was twenty-nine—eighteen years later.

It should be noted here that Levi H. Dowling's popular book *The Aquarian Gospel* is now known to be derived from Notovitch's work. Published in 1908, just fourteen years after Notovitch published *The Unknown Life*, Levi claimed his book was a psychic document, given to him by revelation. Naturally the academic world was skeptical and claimed it was simply plagiarism. With a few embellishments and Levi's personal beliefs infiltrating the book, it largely tells the same story as Notovitch's authoritative work.

According to the ancient manuscripts found by Notovitch, Jesus spent six years learning and teaching the scriptures of India (the Vedas) in Benares, Jagannath Puri, and other cities in the state of Orissa. It was there that his philosophy began to take shape. Although he found great value in Vedic knowledge, he saw how such knowledge could be misused. For instance, the brahmin priests—the intellectual class—were exploiting the lower classes, especially the Shudras, teaching that the knowledge of the Vedas was only for the upper crust. Jesus found this repugnant. Love of God was for every man, woman and child.

Jesus took it upon himself to rectify the situation, and he began teaching Vedic knowledge to the Shudras. Thus he began his activities as a religious reformer, which would make history as he applied it when he returned to the West. There, the Pharisees were teaching a legalistic religion. Jesus reminded them of the spirit behind the law.

In Notovitch's work, too, we see Jesus warning the caste-conscious brahmins that they have forgotten the true teachings of the

Vedas. The Vedas taught the principle of class distinction. But this was originally according to qualification and work. In Orissa, at the time, the whole concept had become distorted, and people were claiming caste rights according to birthright. If one was born in a brahmin family, he was considered a brahmin—even if he lacked the necessary qualifications, such as cleanliness, austerity, mercy, and truthfulness. Jesus sought to put an end to this hypocrisy.

The original Vedic idea, however, was fully accepted by Jesus, and history relates how he incorporated these ideas when he returned to Palestine. Every human being, Jesus taught, should worship God according to his capacity and work. This concept is decidedly Vedic, wherein everyone—according to capacity and work—fit into particular categories or "castes" naturally. And these castes were considered equal in that they facilitated a particular kind of service to the Supreme. Some fit into the intellectual caste (*brahmin*); others are administrators (*kshatriya*); some are inclined toward mercantile activity (*vaishya*); while still others fit into the working class category (*shudra*). But all were equal in the eyes of God.

No wonder, therefore, we find Jesus castigating the "brahmins" for their misrepresentation of Vedic knowledge: They were not actually brahmins, at least not by qualification and spiritual understanding. Indeed, the British would criticize the caste system nineteen hundred years later for a similar reason.

Either due to pure ignorance or impure motivation, the brahmins of Orissa plotted against Jesus' life, again indicating that they were not actually brahmins (It is against the brahminical code to kill in any way, shape or form whatsoever. This is extended to the point that most brahmins are strict vegetarians.) After several unsuccessful attempts on the life of Jesus, we find the master fleeing Jagannath Puri, never to return again.

The Issa story informs us that, after escaping, Jesus journeyed to Nepal, deep into the Himalayas. There he spent another six years teaching the science of spirituality. Onward to Persia, where he preached against the concept of two gods, one of good and one of evil. Denouncing the concept as a primitive form of polytheism, Jesus was not well-received by the Zoroastrians, who believed in the battle between the two gods. "There is only one God," Jesus (Issa) taught, "and that is our Father in heaven."

The next part of the Issa manuscript (and thus Notovitch's book) is almost exactly the same as the Bible account with which we are familiar, complete with Pontius Pilate, the crucifixion, and the Apostles. Thus, what the ancient Buddhist manuscript offers is a possible explanation of Jesus' activities during the eighteen missing years, of which the Bible says nothing.

At this point most readers will probably maintain their initial skepticism. After all, except for the word of a Buddhist monk and a Russian traveller, there is no concrete evidence that the manuscript actually exists, or that its contents are true. What's more, most readers are probably unsure as to whether travel between Palestine and India was possible in those days. Furthermore, and perhaps most importantly, just why would Jesus want to go to India anyway? These are the subjects we will now address.

While it may be difficult to ascertain the authenticity and validity of the Issa manuscript, it is not impossible. In fact, even the Church's attitude on the subject is enlightening. When confronted with the subject by Notovitch, they backed off. Sometimes posing arguments and other times simply ignoring his work, they always seemed fearful, as if they had something to hide, some secret to protect.

According to Elizabeth Clare Prophet, Cardinal Rotelli opposed Notovitch's work because he felt it was "premature," that the world was not ready to hear it. "The Church suffers already too much from the new wave of atheistical thought," Rotelli said to Notovitch. The cardinal was obviously fearful of losing followers who were already skeptical of Church doctrine. They didn't need another obstacle to overcome.

In Rome, Notovitch displayed his version of the Issa manuscript before a cardinal who was close to the Pope. "What would be the good of publishing this?" the nervous prelate offered. "You will make yourself a crowd of enemies. If it be a question of money that interests you..." Notovitch did not take the bribe. He published his book instead.

As time passed, Notovitch was to find that the Vatican library contained sixty-three manuscripts which refer to the Issa story— antique documents which were brought to Rome by Christian missionaries preaching in China, Egypt, Arabia and India. "No wonder that Church official acted funny," Notovitch is said to have realized, "the Issa story is not something new to them!" Notovitch further speculated that one of those missionaries to India might even have been St. Thomas, who according to the *Catholic Encyclopedia*, evangelized India and all quarters from the Persian Gulf to the Caspian Sea.

This brings us again to the question of first century travel between Palestine and India. The apocryphal Acts of Thomas describe the Apostle as preaching the gospel and performing miracles in "the land of the Ganges." What's more, Notovitch was quick to point out, Thomas could not have preached in his native Greek, or even in Hebrew, for the people of India only spoke various dialects of Pali and Sanskrit. So it is entirely probable that he learned the language and even had something to do with the Issa manuscript (being one of the only followers of Jesus in India at the time).

As far as Thomas' preaching in India in the first century, it is beyond doubt. Scholars have conclusively proven that there were trade routes connecting East and West, routes commonly frequented. Land routes reached North India (where Issa travelled), while the sea routes approached the south. Thus no one denies that Thomas ostensibly preached in India. As it was possible for him, it was possible for Jesus.

There is, however, even more conclusive evidence for Thomas' travels in the Orient. According to scholar William Steuart McBirnie in his book *The Search For The Twelve Apostles*, "It has already been pointed out that the sea route to South India was well used in Roman times for the purpose of the pepper trade, and that Roman gold and silver coins from the early centuries of our era have been discovered in Malabarese (South Indian) soil. Moreover, startling numismatic evidence has established the existence of both King Gondophares and his brother Gad as historic figures and not simply legendary characters. Their names have been found on excavated coins and in a Gandhara inscription fixing their rule at about 19-45 A.D. in Scytho-India in the Indus valley." According to the Acts of Thomas, the Apostle travelled to India with a King Gondophares, who had a brother named Gad. Modern scholarship thus endorses the contention that Thomas went to India. The Roman Catholic Church, in fact, now considers the Cathedral of St. Thomas at Mylapur (a suburb of Madras) to be a Basilica, acknowledging that it stands over the tomb of the Apostle. He was buried in India after dying the death of a martyr.

As a matter of fact, Issa's tomb is also allegedly in India, for the Kashmir hypothesis contends that Jesus returned to India after the crucifixion. "What?" the believing Christian will ask. "Our theology teaches that Jesus died on the cross for our sins! Only by this sacrifice can we be saved!"

It may raise some Christian eyebrows, however, to become aware of these little known facts of life: Pope John XXIII openly declared in 1960 that it was through Christ's blood that man was saved and that his death was inessential for this purpose. In other words, the Kashmir hypothesis does not necessarily contradict Christian dogma. Jesus may have been crucified—but he didn't have to die on the cross.

With this in mind, we should review the idea of Jesus dying in Kashmir and see what light it sheds on the life of Saint Issa. As mentioned earlier, German journalist A. Faber-Kaiser was so convinced about the hypothesis that he wrote a penetrating book, *Jesus Died in Kashmir*, which thoroughly explains the whole Issa story (before and after the crucifixion).

According to the account, Jesus survived the crucifixion and again travelled East, this time under the name Yuz Asaf. Settling in Kashmir, the story goes, Jesus married and died a natural death in his old age. A community of Jews in Shrinagar, the capital of Kashmir, still show great reverence toward an old crypt where for generations they have believed Jesus—or Issa, as they call him—is buried.

The premise of Faber-Kaiser's book is quite substantial, supported by Notovitch's work, complex biblical interpretations, and very early Arabic texts. The Koran itself, in fact, clearly states that Jesus did not die on the cross: "They did not kill him, they did not crucify him; it only seemed to them to be so." (Koran, 155-7) Later, Muslim historian Imam Abu Ja'far Muhammad at-Tabri commented, "Isa and his mother, Mary, had to leave Palestine and travel to a distant land, wandering from country to country." The Kashmir hypothesis thus serves to harmonize Christianity and Islam, settling centuries-old disputes. The Christians say Jesus was crucified. The Muslims say he did not die on the cross. The Kashmir hypothesis offers a possible explanation which accommodates both the Christian and Muslim perspectives.

There is more compelling evidence. *Jesus Died in Kashmir* includes sixteen pages of impressive charts, wherein linguistic parallels are drawn between place, tribal, and caste names from Kashmir and those found in the Bible. Further, Faber-Kaiser refers to the ancient *Bhavishya Purana* (part of the Vedic canon), which was written in

Sanskrit 5,000 years ago by the sage Vyasadeva. As a scripture which includes prophesy, it is on a par with the Bible. Faber-Kaiser paraphrases from the *Purana*, "[Maharaja] Shalewahin went out one day to walk in the mountains, and in Voyen, near Shrinagar, saw a distinguished person dressed in white and with a fair complexion. The [Maharaja] asked him his name. Jesus answered that he was known as the son of God and was born of a virgin. The [Maharaja] was surprised, but Jesus explained that he was telling him the truth and that his mission was to purify religion. When the [Maharaja] renewed his questioning, Jesus told him that he had proclaimed his ministry in a country far beyond the Indus, and the people had made him suffer. He had preached of love, the truth and purity of heart, and that for this reason he was known as the Messiah." In this same *Bhavishya Purana*, Jesus also mentions preaching in the land of "the Amalekites," which is decidedly connected to the biblical tradition.

All prophesy in the *Purana*, it may be noted, is worded as if the event had already transpired, and this is a common device in prophetic literature. Still, the actual scenario mentioned above did not occur until three thousand years later, that is to say two thousand years ago. Thus, even the Vedic literature has some mention of the Issa story, proclaiming that Jesus did in fact travel to India.

Notovitch was convinced of these facts. But Swami Abhedananda, a noted disciple of Ramakrishna, was not. In fact, he was quite skeptical. And in 1922 he decided to trek into the arctic region of the Himalayas. He had briefly heard of Notovitch's exploits and, as a scholar, he had to find out for certain. Did the Issa manuscripts actually exist? Or was Notovitch a fraud, as many Church authorities (and Abhedananda himself) were inclined to believe. The Swami went in search of a manuscript.

The results were startling. When he returned, he published a book of his travels, entitled *Kashmiri O Tibetti*. The book tells of his visit to the Buddhist monastery and how he had the Issa manuscript read to him and translated into his native Bengali. Abhedananda soon realized that his text was almost exactly like the work of Notovitch. He was now a believer.

It may be noted that both Notovitch and Abhedananda had to have the transcript translated. They could not read the Pali manuscript themselves. Scholars were thus skeptical upon their return to the West. The two enthusiastic researchers may have been sincere—but what if there was a mistake in the translation? Or what if the Buddhist monks had deceived them?

This problem—however insubstantial—was settled once and for all by a father and son research team. In 1925, artist, philosopher, and distinguished scientist, Nicholas Roerich set out for the Himalayas on an expedition. Amazingly, with no connection to Notovitch and Abhedananda, he came upon the Issa manuscript. What's more, Roerich's son, George, who happened to be travelling with him, was proficient in various Indian dialects, including Pali. They read the manuscript firsthand, took notes, and recorded it in their travel diary. Although at the time they didn't realize its value, years later the value of this diary became apparent.

According to Elizabeth Clare Prophet, "Nicholas Roerich's Central Asiatic Expedition lasted four and a half years. In that time he travelled from Sikkim through the Punjab and into Kashmir, Ladakh, Karakorum, Khotan, and Irtysh, then over the Altai Mountains and through the Oyrot region into Mongolia, Central Gobi, Kansu and Tibet." After all of his travels, Roerich was prompted to write, "We were touched at how widespread is the story of Issa."

While it remains a question for the West, Issa lives in the hearts of the Indian people. And that's a fact that can't be ignored. The Bible concludes: "...and there are also many other things which Jesus did [i.e.—not mentioned in the Bible] the which, if they should be written every one, I suppose that even the world itself could not contain the books that should be written..."

Postcript

While the reader may be ready to admit that Jesus could have feasibly travelled to India, we are left with the question posed earlier: Why would he want to go? There are many superficial reasons which come to mind immediately, and they can be easily understood. Some say he was searching for the three wise men, who, it may be remembered, came from the East. Faber-Kaiser speculates that Jesus was looking for the ten lost tribes of Israel. Others say that, due to persecution, Jesus and Mary, along with St. Thomas, fled for a land that might be richer in understanding, a land of tolerance and peace.

Although any and all of these answers may be true, this author contends that the issue runs deeper, that Jesus, who was preaching an entirely metaphysical doctrine, was searching for a land steeped in spirituality. The Jews were concerned with the here-and-now. But Jesus, unlike most Jewish teachers, claimed that his kingdom was not in the material world but in the Kingdom of God, in heaven. India's teachings, disparaged as "otherworldly" by Jewish critics, was more in line with the mystical teachings of Jesus.

Furthermore, Jesus exhibited certain mystic powers which, although uncommon in the West, were well-known to the yogis of India. For instance, Jesus, it is said, walked on water. But the yogic power known as *laghima siddhi* could also make one lighter than air, so one could, in fact, walk on water. Jesus multiplied the bread and the fish, just as yogis were known to multiply their own forms *(kamavasayita siddhi)* as well as bring all kinds of objects—including bread and fish—from distant places *(prapti siddhi)*. Jesus escaped from his tomb which was blocked by a huge boulder; yogis were able to become smaller than the smallest *(anima siddhi)* to escape from demons. These miracles were not uncommon in ancient India, and Jesus' miracles are too closely related to that of India's yogis for one to assume that it is coincidental. Thus, a comparative study of Vedic philosophy and Christian history, under a bona-fide spiritual master, very quickly reveals the unexcelled knowledge and spiritual profundity of the East, and its influence on the West.

Writer Alex Kack, in an informative feature article in *EASTWEST Journal* (January, 1978), said it most eloquently, "Jesus' journey symbolizes the quest for wisdom, the search for wholeness. The East, then as now, signified the mysterious half of the soul, the hidden consciousness, the higher mind, the intuitive dimension of the psyche which mainstream Greek and Hebrew civilizations de-emphasized or ignored."

This doesn't necessarily mean that Jesus himself was in search of wisdom and wholeness. As the Son of God, he may have indeed been perfect from birth. But as the Messiah, the perfect teacher, Jesus was pointing the way. For those of us in search of the Absolute Truth, Jesus pointed East. Even as the sun rises over the Orient, the Eastern light comes back to us, who wait patiently in the West.

(Originally published as a booklet that was distributed throughout North America in 1984.)

VEDIC PROPHETIC WISDOM
Was Mohammed Predicted?

AN INTERVIEW WITH STEVEN ROSEN, THE EDITOR OF *THE JOURNAL OF VEDIC HERITAGE,* ON JANUARY 2, 1984.

Steve, can you tell me how and why you developed an interest in Hinduism? Being an American, it seems rather strange how much knowledge you have concerning Indian culture. One doesn't often encounter such a thing in the West.

SR: Well, it's not really *Hinduism* that I'm interested in. What I'm attracted to is *Sanatan Dharma,* the eternal religion of the soul. "Hinduism" may appear similar because the last vestiges of Vedic culture (the culture that espoused *Sanatan Dharma*) can be found therein. However, true *Dharma* has nothing to do with sectarian religion.

"Hinduism" can mean almost anything. Specifically, it is a name tagged onto the people of India who engage in a particular set of rites and rituals, although these rituals may manifest in hundreds of different ways. One would be at a disadvantage if one were forced to give a solid definition of Hinduism; a singlular definition just doesn't fit.

First of all, one should know that the word *Hindu* is nowhere to be found in the Vedic literature, India's ancient scriptural texts. The word is a faulty designation borne of the Arab/Muslim era in India, which began in the sixth century and culminated in Akbar's Mogul Empire. The Arab Muslims referred to all people living east of the Sindhu River (now called the Indus) as *Sindhus*. However, because their particular dialect did not allow the "S" sound to be properly pronounced, the word *Sindhu* came out of their mouths as *Hindu*. Since that time the loose lable Hindu has been applied to practically anyone living in India who is not a convert to Christianity or Islam (or Sikhism or Jainism or Buddhism), and the tag "Hindu religion" has been used to describe a potpourri of religious, cultural, and nationalistic activities that happen to have arisen in India.

But "Vedic culture" is beyond all temporary designations. Externally, one may be a Hindu, Muslim, Jew, Christian, or whatever—but he may still benefit from Vedic knowledge. It is transcendental to sectarian concerns.

Originally, all the world benefitted from Vedic knowledge. Gradually, as the present age set in, Vedic culture was narrowed down. Thus we are familiar with it as an "Indian" phenomenon. But now, as the age becomes more and more degraded, we find that even in India many are unaware of its universal application and its all-pervading history. Very few people are now aware of what Vedic culture was originally like; Hinduism is now predominant.

I hope this clears up the difference between Vedic culture and Hindu culture. Hindu culture grew out of Vedic culture in the same way that Christianity grew out of Judaism. Today, Judaism and Christianity are two completely different things. So, too, are Hinduism and Vedic culture.

You see, it is *spirituality* that I am interested in—not the outer shell.

Yes. I understand. But why the Vedic literature? Why not the Bible?
SR: The Bible and the Koran are just fine. I study them, and I derive great inspiration from them. But the Vedas are more comprehensive, and a comparative study reveals this quite readily.

For instance, there are abridged and unabridged dictionaries. That is not to say that the abridged dictionary is *wrong*. It is simply less informative.

Similarly, the Bible and Koran explain that God is great, but only in the Vedas is His greatness explained with any detail. The Bible and the Koran both allude to a spiritual kingdom, but the Vedas alone *describe* this kingdom and its various manifestations. The Western religious literature explains that God is everywhere, but from the Vedas we learn *how* God is everywhere, how He expands, by His Paramatma feature, into every atom. For one who is serious about discovering the nature of God, the Vedas offer a great deal.

Of course, many are more interested in official affiliation with some religion than in finding out the ultimate goal of all religions. For such people, what can be done? The sincere will pick up the truth—wherever he finds it.

I agree with that.
SR: Yes. Chanakya Pandit has said that an intelligent man will take gold even if he finds it in a dirty place. So, even if one is dubious about accepting knowledge from an apparently 'alien' culture, if it indeed rings 'true,' it should be accepted.

Steve, many people are talking about prophecy these days. The Bible is full of all kinds of prophecy—from the coming of Jesus to Armageddon. Do the Vedas contain prophecy?
SR: The prophecy contained in the Vedas would boggle your mind! There is not only prophecy of upcoming sages and Incarnations of God, but also of the present age and forthcoming ages as well. And, unlike the Bible this is all explained in detail.

Your question is very interesting. You see, one of the many reasons the biblical literature is accepted as holy scripture (by Jews, Christians and Muslims) is because of prophecy. After all, many people reason, if a given piece of literature can accurately predict forthcoming events, especially of a Divine nature, that literature is worthy of veneration—and so are the sages who compile it. It is, then, obviously supernatural.

And yet the same people who claim such things about the Bible are in complete ignorance in regard to the Vedas and the Puranas.

In the Puranic section of the Vedas, especially the *Bhavishya Purana*, future events are dictated freely. This literature is thousands of years old—compiled in ancient Sanskrit—and yet it predicts an unlimited number of past, current and future events.

In fact, there is a nice *shloka* about the coming of Mohammed (This can be found in *Parva* 3, *Khand* 3, *Adhya* 3 *Shlokas* 5-6):

> *etan mitrantare mleccha*
> *acaryena samanvitah*
> *Mahamad iti Khyatah*
> *Siyyagrasva samanvitah*

"An illiterate teacher will come along, Mohammed by name, and he will give religion to his fifth-class companions."

Note that Mohammed is mentioned by name! This is the standard. And an interesting point is that only in the Vedas will you find a prediction about a prophet from another part of the world. This is unique to the Vedic revelation. Other scriptures may predict prophets from within their own tradition, but in the Vedic tradition it is universal, predicting self-realized souls from Jesus to Mohammed. The Vedas even describe prophets *on other planets*—so it becomes clear that the Vedas are universal.

This is very interesting.
SR:Yes, but there's more. Twenty-five hundred years before His appearance, *Shrimad-Bhagavatam* ("the ripened fruit of the Vedic tree of Knowledge") predicted the coming of Buddha. And the *Bhagavatam* mentions His parents and place of birth:

> *tatah kalau sampravrte*
> *Sammohaya sura-dvisham*
> *buddho namnanjana-suta*
> *Kikatesu bhavishyati*

"In the beginning of Kali-yuga (the present age), the Personality of Godhead will appear in the province of Gaya as Lord Buddha, the son of Anjana, to bewilder the demons who are always envious of the devotees."

Note the word *"bhavishyati"* in this verse ("will appear"). This indicates that this event was to take place in the future. And indeed it did. That *shloka* was spoken 5,000 years ago, and Buddha appeared 2,500 years after that—or 2,500 years ago.

The *Bhagavatam* predicts partial and total annihilations. It even predicts the hairstyles men will prefer. It simply has to be read to be believed.

Perhaps the most important prediction in the Vedic literature, though, is the coming of Shri Chaitanya Mahaprabhu, for His mission was to establish the yuga-dharma, the process of self-realization for the age.

And what is the recommended process of this age?
SR: The chanting of the holy names of the Lord.

Where in the Vedic literature is Shri Chaitanya and His mission predicted?
SR: Well, in the *Chaitanyopanishad* section of the *Atharva Veda* there are numerous predictions. For example:

> *eko devah sarva-rupi mahatma*
> *gauro-rakta-syamala-sveta-rupah*
> *caitanyatma sa vai caitanya-saktir*
> *bhaktakaro bhaktido bhakti-vedyah*

"The one Supreme Personality of Godhead, Who is the master of all transcendental potencies, and Who may be known only by devotional service, appears in innumerable forms. He has appeared in red, white and black complexions, and He shall also appear in Golden form as Shri Chaitanya Mahaprabhu. He will assume the role of a perfect devotee, and He will teach all souls the path of devotional service." (*Chaitanyopanisad*, text 6)
Also, in the *Vayu Purana*:

> *Kalau sankirtanarambhe*
> *bhavishyami sachi-sutah*

"I shall descend in the Kali-Yuga to inaugurate the *Sankirtan* movement [the movement of congregational chanting]. Specifically, I will descend as the son of Mother Sachidevi." In this way, there are many accurate predictions. Vedic prophecy was being fulfilled before the Bible was even composed.

What do you think of Shripad Shankaracharya's conception of the Vedic philosophy, of merging with the Supreme?
SR: Well, we have to analyze the class of men he was teaching. At that time, Buddhism was predominant in India. And we should not take Shankara's teaching out of historical context.
Buddha drove the Vedas out of India, minmizing the importance of the Vedic literature. This was because people were misinterpreting Vedic texts, killing animals and sacrificing them to "the gods."
Shankara meant to reestablish Vedic authority, but because of his audience—neo-Buddhistic impersonalists—he had to establish the

Vedas in a way that they would undertand, in perverted fashion. This he did. Then, gradually, with the help of Madhvacharya, Ramanujacharya and, ultimately, Shri Chaitanya, the original Vedic teaching became reestablished.

So Shankara's impersonalism (merging with the Supreme) was an emergency teaching, to reestablish Vedic authority. A stopgap solution. But ultimately—and Shankara was well aware of this—the impersonal effulgence of the Lord is subservient to the personal form of the Lord Himself. This is confirmed in *Bhagavad-gita*: *brahmano hi pratishtaham* ("I am the basis of the impersonal Brahman.")

Steve, if you could live anywhere in India, where would you want to live?

SR: Well, Vrindavan is, of course, transcendentally wonderful. I have for a long time fantasized living on Chatikar Road, which has now been renamed Bhaktivedanta Swami Marg, after my Guru Maharaj.

Then, again, Rupa Goswami *has* revealed that Radha-Kunda is the most wonderful place in all the three worlds. Still, Mathura has special attraction for me. This stems from the fact that it is Lord Krishna's birthplace.

"The great city of Mathura has issued from the body of Lord Krishna. Simply by seeing Mathura, one's life becomes successful." (*Garga Samhita*, 25.14)

According to the *Uttara Khanda* of Valmiki *Ramayana*, Mathura was founded by Shatrughna, the younger brother of Lord Rama. During the Treta-yuga, the area was ruled by the demon Madhu Daitya who, along with his son Lavana, made the mistake of challenging the authority of Lord Ramachandra. Lord Rama, who is the all-pervading Vishnu Himself, sent Shatrughna to deal with the two wicked *asuras* Madhu and Lavana. After defeating them in battle, Shatrughna founded the city. It was called at that time Madhupuri, but later Mathura—both names are derived from the demon Madhu. Later, Mathura came under the control of the kings of the Yadu dynasty, the same royal line into which Krishna was later to appear.

Mathura is praised as the "supreme abode" in the *Padyavali* of Shri Rupa Goswami. Mathura is also famous as the place where Lord Krishna first manifested Himself before the eyes of the world. Much later, after the Lord departed for His own abode, Arjuna established Krishna's great grandson Vajranabha on the throne of Mathura. Although Lord Krishna left the planet five thousand years ago, at the dawn of the Kali-yuga, to this day millions of people from all over the world pilgrimage yearly to His birth place in Mathura. They remember Krishna as the internal guide and speaker of the *Bhagavad-gita*.

The *Bhakti Rasamrita Sindhu* states that whoever gives up this holy abode of Mathura and seeks sensual pleasure elsewhere will be forever condemned to wander in the cycle of birth and death under the grip of the illusory material nature. And the *Mathura Khand* of the *Skanda Purana* goes on to say, "It is possible to count the particles of dust on the face of the earth, but the holy places situated within Mathura cannot be counted." In the *Chaitanya Charitamrita*, Krishnadas Kaviraj Goswami says that residing in Mathura is one of the five most effective processes of devotional service. The other four listed are associating with devotees, chanting regularly the holy name of the Lord, hearing the *Shrimad Bhagavatam*, and faithfully worshipping the Deity. Krishnadas Kaviraj promises, "Even a slight performance of these will awaken *Krishna prema*, or love for Krishna." (C.C. *Madhya* 22.129)

Today Mathura has grown into a crowded city of 132,000 persons. Actually, that's according to the 1972 census. Today about one tenth of all the people living within the 168 mile area of Vrajamandala live in Mathura. It is the central city in the Mathura District, being a rail and road junction as well as a market center for the cereals, cotton, oilseeds, and sugarcane grown in the surrounding area. The historic Grand Trunk Road which starts in Peshawat (now in Pakistan) and ends in Calcutta, runs through Mathura.

There are three places of major importance which pilgrims genrerally visit in Mathura, namely, Lord Krishna's birthplace, Vishram ghat, and the temple of Lord Dwarakadish. So, I think, that is where I'd like to live.

Of course, Shridham Mayapur, in West Bengal, is equally transcendental. And the more I think about it, the more I would like to live in close proximity to where Shri Chaitanya Mahaprabhu took His appearance. However, all places become relishable when one engages in the Lord's devotional service. Vrindavan and Mayapur are right here—but one must know how to perceive them. Thus, I am happy living right here in New York, where I can serve the Lord most efficaciously.

(Originally appeared in *The Journal of Vedic Heritage*, No. 3, 1984.)

JAYADEV GOSWAMI:POET
FOR LIBERATED SOULS

S hrila Vyasadeva compiled the Vedic literature some five thousand years ago, and since then many great devotees have created literary works following the conclusions of Vyasadeva's writings and drawing on their own realizations. One such pure devotee was Jayadev Goswami, who in the twelfth century A.D., composed *Gita-govinda*, one of the greatest Vaishnava classics of all time.

Jayadev was born in the village of Kenduli, West Bengal. His father's name was Bhojadeva, and his mother's Rama. Little is known about his early life, but it is said that he was a Sanskrit scholar at an early age and was inclined towards spiritual life. Some of his contemporaries have described him as "the incarnation of melody."

As a young man, Jayadev went to Jagannath Puri after first visiting many holy places. There he married a girl named Padmavati who was devoted to the Deity of Lord Jagannath (Krishna, the "Lord of the Universe"). Jayadev also developed deep love for the Lord. Inspired by the beauty of Puri and Lord Jagannath, he composed *Gita-govinda*, and it quickly became the joy of the Vaishnava community.

At the time, Gajapati Purushottamadev was the provincial king. He was openly envious of Jayadev and soon posed an ill-fated challenge. The king considered himself a master poet, on a par with Jayadev, and composed a book entitled *Abhinava Gita-govinda*, which in fact was a cheap imitation of Jayadev's work. One day, he summoned his advisors and asked them to widely circulate his work in an attempt to make it more popular than Jayadev's. The king's own men, however, ridiculed his attempt, saying that "it is impossible to compare a lamp with the sun."

Still, the king was relentless. A controversy soon arose, and the *brahmanas* (the king's priests) decided that the matter would be settled by placing both manuscripts before the Deity of Lord Jagannath for the night. By morning, they said, the Lord Himself would decide.

When the devotees went to greet the Deity the next day, they found Jayadev's *Gita-govinda* clasped against the Deity's chest, and the king's manuscript scattered about the floor. The decision was clear.

Jayadev's fame spread across India, his work being recited or sung in every major temple and royal court. So popular was his work that beginning in the fifteenth century, various schools of classical Indian art began to render it more than any other religious text. *Gita-govinda* was illustrated in Gujarat, Uttar Pradesh, Rajasthan, and the Punjab hills. Gujarat produced the earliest illustrated manuscript in 1450. The next significant *Gita-govinda* series was painted in 1590, and it is now on display in Bombay's Prince of Wales Museum.

The great Mogul emperor Akbar was an admirer of *Gita-govinda* and commissioned a special illustrated manuscript, one of the most important renditions ever produced. His manuscript was done in Mogul style and showed a fascinating merger of cultural milieus. Lord Krishna's eternal consort, Radharani, for instance, was depicted in typical Mogul dress. This was unorthodox but reflected a certain non-sectarian beauty.

Later in life, Jayadev became the court poet of King Lakshmanasen, the King of Bengal for the latter half of the twelfth century. The king's patronage of Jayadev added insult to injury for Gajapati Purushottamadev, who resigned from his post in Puri.

Jayadev's work became more famous as the years passed, and after he left this world, the words of his immortal *Gita-govinda* were inscribed on the Jaya-Vijaya doorway of the Jagannath temple in Puri.

The most significant testament to the value of Jayadev's work is that it was fully appreciated by Chaitanya Mahaprabhu, who used to have it read to Him nightly. Lord Chaitanya is Krishna Himself in the role of a perfect devotee. Since God Himself is pleased with Jayadev's work, it must be considered consummate.

Consequently, Shrila Prabhupada states that Jayadev should be counted among the *mahajans*, the great souls who come to this world on behalf of the Lord to show proper methods of devotional service. This puts Jayadev in the company of such exalted personalities as Brahma, Narada, and Prahlad.

Jayadev's distinct position, however, is revealed in the depth of his work. *Gita-govinda* deals with the very intimate pastimes of Radha and Krishna, the ultimate in esoteric spiritual truth. Skillfully weaving the facts of pastoral drama with that of the scriptures through the medium of Sanskrit melody, Jayadev brings to life every nuance of spiritual love, both in union and in separation.

Still, as the perfect teacher, Jayadev is careful, for he does not want his readers to mistake the loving pastimes of Radha and Krishna for lusty exchanges. The interaction of Radha and Krishna is the most wholesome spiritual relationship, of which material relationships are but a perverted counterpart.

To prevent misconceptions, great Vaishnava teachers throughout history have recommended the reading of basic spiritual texts, such as the *Bhagavad-gita,* before one approaches the confidential pastimes of Radha and Krishna. And even then, one requires the direction of a bona-fide spiritual master coming in disciplic succession.

Otherwise, one is sure to misinterpret the teachings. Shrila Prabhupada, in fact, has written that the esoteric works of Jayadev and others like him should be read only by liberated souls.

Jayadev begins his *Gita-govinda* with a beautiful prayer, entitled *Dashavatara Stotra*: "Prayer to the Ten Incarnations." In this prayer, he reminds his readers of Lord Krishna's divinity, hoping to allay their possible misinterpretation of the pastimes of the Lord recounted in the book. In the last verse of *Dashavatara Stotra,* Jayadev summarizes the activities of ten incarnations of Lord Krishna:

O Lord Krishna, I offer my obeisances unto You, the Supreme Lord. You appear in the form of the following ten incarnations. In the form of Matsya, You rescue the Vedas, and as Kurma, You bear the Mandara Mountain on Your back. As Varaha, You lift the earth with Your tusk, and in the form of Narasimha, You tear open the chest of Hiranyakashipu. In the form of Vamana, You trick Bali by asking him for only three steps of land, and then You take away the whole universe by expanding Your steps. As Parashurama, You slay all the wicked kings, and as Ramachandra, You conquer the evil king Ravana. In the form of Balaram, You carry a plow, with which You subdue the wicked and draw toward You the river Yamuna. As Lord Buddha, You show compassion to all living beings, and at the end of the present age, Kali-yuga, You appear as Kalki to destroy the lowest among men.

(Originally printed in *Back to Godhead Magazine*, Vol. 24, No. 6)

PRINCES, PANDITS & PROVERBS
The Sayings of Chanakya Pandit

When an old college friend told me he would be teaching a course on proverbs at the New School for Social Research in New York City, I immediately began to think about how I might assist him. Since his major was English literature, he was always ready to come to my rescue when I needed help preparing a college lecture on Krishna consciousness or researching for a literary project. Now I might be able to return the favor.

He had a trepidation about his new course and asked me whether the Vedic tradition offered any insights into the nature of proverbs. In response, I asked him to first explain what exactly he meant by "proverbs." He told me that a proverb is an adage, a simple, short saying that sums up a profound truth.

At first, I thought of the *Vedanta-sutra*, terse codes that express deep philosophical wisdom. But as my friend continued to speak, citing well-known proverbs and their authors, such as Confucius and Lao Tzu, I realized that the works of Chanakya Pandit, whom Shrila Prabhupada quoted in almost every volume he produced, could more fittingly be called proverbs.

Shrila Prabhupada often used Chanakya's sayings, which are revered throughout the Indian subcontinent, to illustrate Krishna conscious ideas. For instance, in *Shrimad Bhagavatam* (1.13.15, purport), Shrila Prabhupada cites Chanakya's advice that valid moral instructions should be accepted even if given by a low-born and unqualified person. Even if gold is covered by stool, says Chanakya, it is still gold.

Shrila Prabhupada taught that Chanakya, a great sage who lived three centuries before Christ, was a *brahmana*, a wise man—he even referred to him as a saint. Although Shrila Prabhupada once pointed out that Chanakya was not, strictly speaking, a pure Vaishnava, from Shrila Prabhupada's writings it is clear that he had great respect for the Pandit's wisdom.

The more I told my friend about Chanakya, the more we both realized that Chanakya's works would add immensely to the proverbs course. And my friend asked me to be a guest speaker when his course was finally underway. Yet my knowledge of Chanakya Pandit as a historical personality left much to be desired. For me, he was mostly an abstraction, a legendary soothsayer my spiritual master frequently quoted. To really help my friend, I needed to do some homework.

We went to the Forty-second Street library to research Chanakya's life and times. Chanakya Pandit, we discovered, is commonly known to historians as Kautilya (although he is also known as Vishnugupta and Vatsyayana). Beyond having composed volumes of proverbs, Chanakya is famous for his *Artha-shastra* ("Treatise on Political Economy") and for counseling King Chandragupta Maurya, one of Alexander the Great's chief adversaries.

Chandragupta is known as Sandrocottus to Greek historians, and he is the founder of the Mauryan dynasty. In the early part of his career, he wandered the Punjab and, along with his countrymen, opposed Alexander's conquering forces. History records that it was Chandragupta's chief advisor, Chanakya Pandit, who was actually responsible for the king's ultimate victory. In *The Minister's Signet Ring,* a work of the sixth century A.D. that purports to describe the last stages of Chandragupta's triumph over Alexander and the Nanda princes, the king himself is depicted as a weak and insignificant youth; the real ruler of the empire was Chanakya.

In 321 B.C. Chandragupta conquered Magadha (South Bihar). He proceeded to annex various parts of northern India and campaigned against the Greek Selsucus Nicator, the former general of Alexander. Under Chanakya's wise counsel, Chandragupta ruled for twenty-four years. The Mauryan Empire, however, lasted some 120 years more, being led first by the founding father's son, Bindusara, and then by his grandson, the famous Emperor Ashoka, who eventually converted to Buddhism.

During the reign of Chandragupta (321-297 B.C.), Chanakya Pandit became widely known for his wisdom and scriptural knowledge. He was a simple and austere man, and deeply religious as well. A contemporary of Aristotle, who was summoned to Macedon to teach Alexander the Great, Chanakya is sometimes compared to the noted Greek philosopher, and at other times he has been compared to Machiavelli, for his *Arthashastra* has many similarities to *The Prince*. Aristotle and Chanakya also have common attitudes toward republican forms of government.

The most amazing thing about Chandragupta and Chanakya Pandit, my friend and I were soon to find out, was that both of them were predicted in the *Shrimad Bhagavatam* (12.1.11,12), which was compiled almost 2,500 years before their time:

nava nandan dvijah kascit
prapannan uddharisyati
tesam abhave jagatim
maurya bhoksyanti vai kalau

"A certain *brahmana* [Chanakya] will betray the trust of King Nanda and his eight sons and will destroy their dynasty. In their absence the Mauryas will rule the world as the age of Kali continues."

sa eva candraguptam vai
dvijo rajye 'bhiseksyati
tat-suto varisaras tu
tatas casokavardhanah

"This *brahmana* will enthrone Chandragupta, whose son will be named Varisara [Bindusara]. The son of Varisara will be Ashokavardhana [Emperor Ashoka]."

These Sanskrit verses fully predict the essential history of the Maurya dynasty, mentioning Chandragupta and his descendants by name. Although Chanakya is not specifically named, there is a clear inference, and Vaishnava commentators, such as Shridhara Swami, Vishvanath Chakravarti Thakur, and, currently, Hridayananda dasa Goswami, say his identification with the *brahmana* alluded to in this text is inescapable.

A great Krishna conscious teacher of the modern age, Shrila Bhaktivinode Thakur (1838-1914), also found this period to be of importance, perhaps owing to the scriptural predictions. In 1857-58, he composed a two-part English epic entitled *Poried*, which he intended to complete in twelve volumes. These two books, written in lucid, melodious English verse, described the wanderings of Porus, who challenged Alexander the Great and was eventually defeated by him. According to the late prominent Indologist A.L. Basham, Porus's name derives from Paurava, which would connect him with the Kuru dynasty, the family upon which the *Mahabharata* centers. Bhaktivinode Thakur's work details the story of Porus and its relation to Chandragupta and Chanakya Pandit. The first of his two published volumes can be found at the British Museum in London.

The Pandit's Proverbs

In the Oriental Division of the huge Forty-second Street Library, my friend and I found the *Chanakya-niti-darpana*, a collection of Chanakya's most famous proverbs. Here are some of my favorites:

"An intelligent person moves on one foot while standing on the other. One should not abandon his previous position without having duly considered a superior position."

I really liked this quote because it reminded me of my early years in Krishna consciousness. Before becoming a devotee, I wanted to be sure that life in Krishna consciousness was everything the devotees said it was. After all, if I was to give up meat-eating, intoxication, illicit sex, and gambling, I wanted to be sure that I was getting something even better in return. I chanted, read Shrila Prabhupada's books, and associated with devotees. In this way, I "duly considered" the superior position of Krishna consciousness.

"One becomes liberated by knowledge, not by shaving the head."

Krishna consciousness is not superficial. Chanakya seeks to warn his audience not to be mere show-bottle renunciants. If a man is going to shave his head (generally a sign of renunciation), he should do it for the right reasons. In addition, Chanakya was not deprecating the shaving of one's head; he himself sported the shaven head and *sikha*, the tuft of hair in the back. A shaven head, while external, can be a sign of one's internal Krishna consciousness.

"What good will it be if a fool studies the scriptures? What good is it for a blind person to use a mirror?"

Again superficiality is rejected. This is perhaps Chanakya's most endearing quality, at least from my perspective. He is not content that someone shaves his head or studies the scriptures. It is spiritual insight which comes form the process of Krishna consciousness and learning in disciplic succession, and it is this which Chanakya hopes to bring out. This separates the saints from the swindlers.

"It is better to give up one's life than to live with a loss of honor. For by giving up the body one experiences only momentary misery, but by living in disgrace one suffers every day."

Here Chanakya explains *shreyas* versus *preyas*, or long-term versus short-term enjoyments. Even in the material world people desire things that last. Most people would rather own a home than rent an apartment. Or they would opt for a long-term relationship rather than a casual fling.

This truth carries greater validity on the spiritual platform. "Of the existent there is no cessation," Krishna says, "and of the nonexistent there is no endurance." In other words, if something is real it will always exist.

A dream, for instance, is considered unreal. Why? Because it comes to an end. Similarly, material life comes to an end, and it is therefore considered illusory. But spiritual life is eternal. For this reason, it is considered real in an ultimate sense.

"A person who gives up things that are certain and pursues things that are uncertain loses both."

Those who understand higher spiritual values reject gambling. Chanakya advises us not to indulge our speculative tendencies. Rather, we should approach a bona fide spiritual master and in this way be certain about the goal of life. The *guru* receives knowledge in a disciplic succession tracing back to Lord Krishna Himself, and thus he is able to give his disciple perfect knowledge. One who receives knowledge in this way can be certain that he will attain spiritual happiness.

"Even one moment of life spent cannot be regained for millions of dollars. Therefore, what greater loss is there than time spent uselessly?"

Useless time is time spent in materialistic pursuits. One cannot kill time; rather, one is killed by time. Krishna in the form of *kala*—"time"—engages all men. He prefers to engage them in direct loving service, and if one is so fortunate as to be directly engaged in such devotional service, Krishna consciousness, then one's time is certainly being spent usefully. And "millions of dollars" cannot come close to the value of even a second in Krishna's service, which has eternal value and unlimited promise.

"One should not trust a wicked person, although he may speak sweet words. Because although there may be honey at the tip of his tongue, there is poison in his heart."

Chanakya Pandit here asserts the importance of being perceptive. One should not be swayed by appearances. As it is said, "Even the devil can quote scripture." In Krishna consciousness, we are taught to not only hear what a person says, but to witness his actions as well. The scriptures make it quite clear that a saintly person behaves in a particular way. Chanakya concurs, warning us not to judge someone merely by the words that emanate from his lips. The genuine saint must not only speak about God but must also live a life of devotional service to Him.

"Virtuous persons and fruit-laden trees bow, but fools and dry sticks break because they do not bend."

Bowing before one's superiors and especially before the Deity of the Supreme Lord is a sign of humility, and it helps one remember one's subservient position. If one refuses to do so, it is a reflection of one's arrogance (or ignorance), and it can impede one's spiritual progress.

"A man becomes great not by sitting on some high seat but

through higher qualities. Can a crow become an eagle simply by sitting on top of a palatial building?"

This is again one of Chanakya's famous quotes in which he disparages superficiality and blind acceptance. Krishna consciousness is a science, and an adherent is encouraged to use logic and reason as much as faith and devotion. Just because someone adopts the posture of a big *guru* on a high seat doesn't mean he is a qualified spiritual master. The actual qualifications are detailed in the scriptures and by previous saints and sages.

"The sounding of the *mridanga* [drum] in the *kirtan* is proclaiming loudly that those who have no devotion to Lord Krishna are very shameful and reprehensible. This is so because the *mridanga* sounds '*dhiktam, dhiktam,*' which means 'Oh, great shame! Oh, great shame!'"

Herein Chanakya expresses his devotion to the Supreme Person, Lord Shri Krishna. Using a Sanskrit rhetorical device, the Pandit wittily shows the great shame in wasting one's life outside the service of the Supreme Lord.

Thus reflecting on Chanakya's proverbs in the light of Shrila Prabhupada's teachings, I felt ready to lecture at my friend's proverbs class. Armed with a storehouse of Shrila Prabhupada's insights into the real meaning behind them, I felt that the hardest part of my work was already done.

(Originally appeared in *Back to Godhead Magazine*, Vol. 23, No. 8.)

6

WHO IS SHRILA PRABHUPADA?

History is replete with examples of good conquering evil. Lord Buddha, it is said, vanquished the demon Mara; Jesus Christ was victorious over Satan; Allah defeated Iblis; Ahurmazda conquered Ahriman; in the Vedic literature Krishna destroys the enemies of the righteous—Putana, Aghasura, Bakasura, the Keshi demon and, finally, Kamsa.

But perhaps the greatest example of righteous victory has occurred in our own day and age. His Divine Grace A.C. Bhaktivedanta Swami Prabhupada has declared an all-out war on illusion and ignorance. His years of hard work and pure devotion have left an indelible mark on the face of illusion and ignorance personified, giving her a sour expression indeed.

While a fortunate few are aware of this phenomenon, the mass of people are oblivious to it. Shrila Prabhupada's work is relatively unknown, especially when one considers the magnitude of his triumph. To be sure, the illusory energy is still a formidable foe. But Shrila Prabhupada, through writing books, establishing temples, and training followers in the detailed science of Krishna consciousness, has created an equally formidable shelter, a respite from the world of illusion. And one who takes this shelter seriously will never be troubled by the evil of ignorance or illusion again. He will emerge victorious.

What follows is a short biographical sketch of the person who made this possible. Naturally, in an abbreviated version of such an illustrious life story, many important facts and events will be obscured (or downright omitted!). But one need not miss out on these indispensable pastimes. The author requests his readers to consult the books of Shrila Satsvarupa Dasa Gosvami, especially his *Shrila Prabhupada-lilamrita*, which explains Shrila Prabhupada's life story with depth, clarity, precision, and pure devotion.

His Divine Grace Shrila Prabhupada took his birth in Calcutta, India, in 1896. He had pure Krishna conscious parents. His father's name was Gour Mohan De; his mother's, Rajani. The boy was called Abhay Charan, although he was sometimes called Nandu, because he was born on the day immediately following Krishna's birthday celebration (Nandotsav).

Shrila Prabhupada's early childhood was steeped in Krishna culture. From his earliest childhood he was extremely fond of Lord Krishna and the Ratha-yatra Festival, and he would regularly stage his own miniature Ratha-yatras. Although he preferred playing his small *mridanga* (a clay drum used for devotional songs) to going to school, his mother's counsel prevailed, and he went on to exhibit extraordinary ability as a student. He excelled in all subjects and was particularly keen in oral expression, debate, and discussion.

He completed his studies in philosophy, economics, and English at Calcutta's Scottish Churches College, and shortly thereafter he became dedicated to the cause of Mahatma Gandhi.

In 1965, at age sixty-nine, His Divine Grace left India for America with only forty rupees. In 1966 he founded the International Society for Krishna Consciousness (ISKCON) in New York City, and in the decade that followed, he established some 108 temples in major cities around the world.

Many thus revere Shrila Prabhupada as India's greatest scholar, philosopher, prophet, and cultural ambassador. According to the 1976 Encyclopedia Britannica Book of the Year, he "astonished academic and literary communities worldwide by writing and publishing fifty-two books on the ancient Vedic culture...in the period from October 1968 to November 1975."

What Prabhupada had achieved in twelve years is unparalleled in all of world history. His Divine Grace now has tens of thousands of full-time initiated followers of all races and ages. And he is officially recognized as the most recent teacher in the prestigious lineage of masters known as the Brahma Madhva Gaudiya Sampradaya, being the twenty-eighth major teacher in this line since Vyasa, the compiler of the Vedic literature. Shrila Prabhupada also formed his "Governing Body Commission" (GBC) to manage his society and to make sure that it strictly adheres to the principles of the disciplic succession.

By 1977, in the brief span of twelve years, the International Society had spread to six continents. During that period His Divine Grace circled the globe fourteen times—writing, translating, lecturing and personally guiding his disciples all the while. By his instruction and his example he showed them how to become self-realized and how to place Vedic knowledge within easy reach of every man, woman and child on this planet.

As of March, 1977, fifty-five million copies of Shrila Prabhupada's renderings of India's spiritual classics had seen print, with forty-three million copies published in English alone. His books are now being used in ninety percent of North America's universities and thousands of public libraries throughout the world. Hundreds of professors worldwide have reviewed his books, which are now being published in twenty-six major languages. Shrila Prabhupada's *Back to Godhead* magazine still has a strong monthly circulation (after forty-two years of publication), and it is increasing regularly.

The many Vedic farm communities based on the principle of cow protection, which Shrila Prabhupada has established throughout the world, are thriving both economically and spiritually. Their basic principle has always been what Prabhupada called "plain living and high thinking." which is a central theme in Vedic philosophy.

Started by Prabhupada many years ago, several building projects are now well established, and new projects are beginning at regular intervals. Current projects are underway in Bombay, Hyderabad, Mayapur (West Bengal), Kurukshetra, Shri Lanka, and Vrindavan.

The children of Shrila Prabhupada's disciples get their education in Gurukulas throughout the world. In addition, Sunday schools have been established in the West for the children of the Indian community. This project is Prabhupada's method of enabling Indians living abroad to keep their Indian culture vibrantly alive.

Presenting fine and performing arts in the West was another of

Shrila Prabhupada's major concerns. A multimedia diorama museum depicting the *Bhagavad-gita* and using many special effects has been established in Los Angeles and Detroit. Also, an art academy was established some sixteen years ago for producing Krishna conscious oil paintings for display and publication in Shrila Prabhupada's books.

For scientists, Shrila Prabhupada established the Bhaktivedanta Institute, a scientific body consisting mostly of his Ph.D. disciples. The Institute's purpose is to conduct scholarly research, present papers, and hold forums for demonstrating the validity of the Vedic conclusions on God, the soul, and the nature of life.

In addition to his other achievements, Shrila Prabhupada has brought India's major cultural and religious festivals to the West. These include Janmashtami, Diwali, Ramnavami, Gaur Purneem, Holi, and Ratha-yatra. The Ratha-yatra Festival is replicated every year in almost perfect detail in San Francisco, Los Angeles, Chicago, New York, Guadalajara, London, Melbourne, and many other cities throughout the world. Although he left this mortal world in November of 1977, his accomplishments live on forever.

Shrila Prabhupada distinguished himself from many other Indian teachers in that he presented himself not as God but as God's servant. He was always critical of self-styled *gurus* who let themselves be worshipped. "These 'gods' are very cheap." Once someone asked him, "Are you God?" and Shrila Prabhupada replied, "No, I am not God—I am a servant of God." Then he paused for a minute and said, "Actually I am not even a servant of God. I am *trying* to be a servant of God. A servant of God is no ordinary thing."

Shrila Prabhupada, of course, was no ordinary person, and he continued writing and translating up to the last moments of his eighty-one-year earthly sojourn. He often quoted the following verse form *Shri Chaitanya Charitamrita*: "One who has taken his birth as a human being in the land of India should make his life successful and work for the benefit of all other people."

Shrila Prabhupada indeed taught that Indian wisdom combined with American resourcefulness could save the world from selfishness and self-destruction. His Divine Grace envisioned a cultural conquest in the West—a peaceful conquest—in which Vedic culture would prevail. In the sixteenth century Shri Krishna Chaitanya Mahaprabhu predicted, "In every town and village of the world, My name—Krishna—will be sung." Shrila Prabhupada has already fulfilled this prophecy, and many thousands share firmly in his conviction that India's Krishna conscious culture will at last bring peace, prosperity, and happiness to every one of us.

Postscript

On November 14th, 1977, at 7:30 P.M. (India time), His Divine Grace A.C. Bhaktivedanta Swami Prabhupada, founder-*acharya* and worldwide leader of the Hare Krishna Society, departed from this world. On account of prolonged illness, Shrila Prabhupada had taken shelter of Lord Krishna's holy land of Vrindavan, where on September 6th he had celebrated his eighty-first birthday. His disciples and followers carry on his mission and continue to spread Krishna consciousness throughout the world.

(Previously unpublished. It was, however, distributed as a tract by the devotees of New York ISKCON in 1986.)

WHOLE LIFE EXPOSÉ

AN ADDRESS AT THE WHOLE LIFE EXPO IN NEW YORK CITY.

Thank you for allowing me to speak at the 1985 Whole Life Expo. I would like to ask you all to reflect for a moment on the implications of the word *whole*. What does it mean to be truly whole? This is what I would like to discuss at the Expo here today.

Everyone can appreciate "holistic life." Some may call it that, some may not. But everyone tries to make his or her life as "whole" as possible. No one likes to live in a fragmented way. Accordingly, we struggle to keep a balance, making sure that there is no lack in our life. We like to feel complete, or whole.

Somehow, we sense that a complete whole is more complete than just the sum of its parts. Indeed, *Webster's Unabridged Dictionary* defines *holistic* in much the same way: "The view that an organic or integrated whole has a reality independent of and greater than the sum of its parts."

And so a thoughtful person is concerned with himself as a whole, his physical, mental, intellectual, and spiritual well-being. If one of these aspects of his personality is out of kilter, it throws his whole system off. He does not feel complete. The struggle for existence is thus largely a struggle for keeping perfect equilibrium among different facets of ourselves as a whole.

The more subtle aspects of our being are more important in regard to our experiencing ourselves in regard to our wholeness. If we have a physical problem—let's say we have a broken leg—that will certainly affect us. But we can still function—and we can function quite well for that matter. Now, if we get more subtle—off the physical platform—and onto the mental platform, a problem can get more serious. Mental equilibrium can affect the whole body—what to speak of the leg. Thus, although bodily maintenance is important, mental and intellectual maintenance is, in a sense, more important.

Subtler than body, mind, and intelligence is the spiritual dimension, the soul. Logically, then, this must be the most important of all. And a holistic concept that neglects the soul is thus not holistic in the true sense of the word. A person who ignores his spiritual side is not whole.

Of course, the goal is to maintain all dimensions of our existence in harmony. But the comparative importance of the spiritual side cannot be denied. After all, we may claim that we are a combination of body, mind, intelligence, and soul—and this is certainly true to some degree. But the body, mind, and intelligence are always changing. We cannot claim to have the same body now that we had when we were youngsters—yet we are the same person. We do not have the same mind or intelligence—yet, again, we are the same person. You are always you. And that "you" must be the one thing that doesn't change. Acknowledging that the body, mind, and intellect are always changing, *you are the soul.*

This soul requires just as much nourishment as does the body, mind, or intelligence. To give great amounts of time to the maintenance of the material body—especially to the exclusion of the soul—is a great waste. One can never be happy like that. It's like cleaning a bird cage and neglecting to feed the bird within. Of course, the bird cage should be kept clean—but why waste time if you are just going to let the bird die? Clean the cage, but feed the bird. Take care of the body, mind, and intelligence, but don't neglect the soul, the spiritual dimension.

Such holistic truths were originally espoused by ancient India's Vedic literature. In the invocation to the *Isopanisad,* the perfection of holistic life is enunciated as is its source:

> *om purnam adah purnam idam*
> *purnat purnam udacyate*
> *purnasya purnam adaya*
> *purnam evavasisyate*

"The Supreme Personality of Godhead is perfect and complete, and because He is completely perfect, all emanations from Him, such as this phenomenal world, are perfectly equipped as complete wholes. Whatever is produced of the complete whole is also complete in itself. Because He is the complete whole, even though so many complete units emanate form Him, He remains the complete balance."

This profound verse clearly explains why we pursue completeness, why we want to be whole. The reason, very simply, is that we are constitutionally whole. It's inherent.

As part of the Supreme Whole, God, we are whole in and of ourselves. This is the nature of spiritual wholeness—it is the exact opposite of so-called material wholeness, which isn't really wholeness at all. For instance, if you take a piece of paper and rip it into little pieces and then you throw all the pieces around the room, you no longer have the original piece of paper. But spiritually it is just the opposite. If you could rip a spiritual piece of paper and throw the pieces all over, the original, whole paper would still exist! This is the way it is with God. Although He expands into innumerable spirit souls, He still remains complete. His original position is not diminished. He remains whole. This is the nature of the Absolute, as opposed to the nature of that which is relative.

And because the spirit souls emanate from the complete Absolute whole, they have a sort of wholeness in themselves. Any quality found in God can be found in the ordinary living entity to some minute degree—hence the Biblical statement that we are made in the image of God. But our wholeness must be considered subordinate to God's. He is infinite, and we are infinitesimal.

One manifestation that shows our wholeness is subordinate to God's is our need to render service. God is wholly independent. We are not. We are dependent on Him for so many things: food, air, fire, rain—even for our body, mind, and intelligence. Our perfect wholeness is exhibited when we render service to that which sustains us.

One hand washes the other, both hands wash the face, and in this way we take care of the rest of the body, knowing full well the importance of our body as a whole. Thus, our hands "glorify" the body in that they work for the benefit or well-being of the whole body. Similarly, the living being begins to nourish himself when he starts to glorify the Lord. When one takes the time to vibrate praises of the Lord, one's overall physical, mental, and intellectual well-being is augmented by genuine spiritual well-being.

The world's original religious scriptures, the Vedic literature, specifically recommend the chanting of the *maha-mantra: Hare Krishna, Hare Krishna, Krishna Krishna, Hare Hare/ Hare Rama, Hare Rama, Rama Rama, Hare Hare*. This is the prayer par excellence, because it asks nothing of God in return. It asks nothing more than to be engaged in the Lord's service: "O Lord! O energy of the Lord! Please engage me in Your service." This prayer contains every aspect of the Absolute Truth and is thus the essence of holistic life in the full sense of the term.

(Originally appeared in *Back to Godhead Magazine*, Vol. 21, No. 4.)

VEGETARIANISM AND
THE WORLD RELIGIONS

WBAI RADIO, JUNE 14, 1987, SHELTON WALDEN'S WORLDWATCH, FEATURING AN INTERVIEW WITH STEVEN ROSEN, AUTHOR OF *FOOD FOR THE SPIRIT—VEGETARIANISM AND THE WORLD RELIGIONS.*

WBAI: Welcome to Worldwatch. This week we'll be talking with Steven Rosen, author of a ground-breaking new book, *Food for the Spirit.* In this work, author Rosen tackles the touchy subjects of diet and religion. Tell our BAI listeners, Steve, why you felt that religionists should be aware of diet, especially in relation to vegetarianism and animal rights.

SR: Well, I think that everyone—not only religionists—should be aware of the importance of proper diet. In fact, it is a biblical command: "And you shall diligently guard your health and life" (*Deut.* 4:15). It has been documented that vegetarians live longer and live healthier than do meat eaters. How can one practice one's religion if one's health is on the wane? So, in this way, the Bible asks us to guard our health. Also, you mentioned "animal rights." Actually, there is another tremendously disregarded biblical command in this regard: *tzar baalay hayyim*. This is Hebrew. It is the mandate to have compassion for animals. And this appears throughout the biblical literature.

The problem of animal abuse, however, is quite widespread. In the United States alone, every year, more than five billion animals are killed for food and 100 million animals are needlessly tortured in research laboratories.

WBAI: I've read similar statistics in vegetarian magazines, such as *Vegetarian Times* and *Animals' Agenda*. How can our listeners know that these facts and figures are not the exaggerations of some predisposed group.

SR: They can know by researching the subject for themselves. This is not simply the concern of some special interest group. Rather, these things have been documented in such prestigious journals as *The Journal of the American Medical Association, The American Journal of Clinical Nutrition* and *The Borden Review of Nutrition Research.*

WBAI: Okay. But back to religion. Do you think, practically, that this is a religious issue? I mean aren't the subjects of diet and religion like apples and oranges? True, there are koshering laws in the Jewish faith and, I suppose, similar things in the other religions. But overall I think most people will say that religion is a matter of faith, not dietary preference.

SR: That's true. But what if one's dietary preference affected one's faith? For instance, religion deals with ethics, morals, compassion, and mercy. As Isaac Bashevis Singer has said, "How can we pray to God for mercy if we are not willing to extend mercy to others?" And this is just common sense. It's simply unfair that we do not extend our sense of mercy to the animals. This is as I have quoted earlier, a biblical precept. Yet we tend to ignore biblical precepts that do not strike our fancy.

Can we be willing to change our hearts but not our diet? The two are inseparable. To claim that these can be separated is sheer hypocrisy! Man does not want to be killed—yet he kills. Man does not want to be the victim of injustice—yet he is unjust. This sort of paradox makes a mockery of religion. The genuine religionist becomes god-like, or godly. As he does not want to be killed, he is careful not to kill others. As he does not want to be the "victim" of a given situation, he does not victimize others. And as he wants God to show him mercy, so also is he merciful to those who are weaker than he. This is fundamental, I think, to real religion. If our diet involves violence—we are setting ourselves up for a nasty future. Violence begets violence. This is the law of *karma*: "For every action, there is an equal and opposite reaction." For this reason, many Eastern traditions embrace vegetarianism. They believe that he who lives by the sword will die by the sword. In the West, we say, "as ye sow, so shall ye reap." In actuality, this is the same as *karma*. Unfortunately, it is rarely extended to the animals or our diet. But in the East it is.

WBAI: Let's start with the Bible. Can you give us a brief synopsis of vegetarianism in the Old Testament? Just a basic outline.

SR: Yes. In the very first chapter of the first book of the Bible, a non-meat diet is recommended. God says, "...I have given you every herb-yielding seed which is upon the face of the earth, and every tree in which is the fruit of a tree-yielding seed—to you it shall be for food. That's *Genesis* 1:29. So God does not beat around the burning bush, as it were. Right in the beginning, He emphasizes the vegetarian diet.

And then He explains that this original, non-meat diet is "very good." This is an expression He reserves only for the vegetarian diet. Later diets containing meat are referred to as "concessions" as opposed to "very good."

WBAI: Okay. But what about those concessions? Much later, I believe, God allows Noah and his descendants the option to eat meat.

SR: Still, if studied in context, it is obvious that this is a question of God's *permissive* will versus His *preferred* will. In other words, God may have allowed this concession. But He never indicated that this diet was preferable. In fact, He seems to indicate rather clearly that it was not.

I think the crucial thing here is to understand exactly what was taking place in the time of Noah. Actually, man had become so depraved that he would eat a limb immediately torn from a living animal. The situation had become so degraded that God had decided to create a great flood. Incidentally, a great flood, as depicted in the Bible, would have undoubtedly destroyed all vegetation—thus, at that time, there was hardly an alternative to animal foods.

Anyway, God did give a concession at that time for eating meat. This occurs in the ninth chapter of *Genesis*, where God gives permission for man to eat everything that moves. Soon after, however, God says that man should still not eat the blood of animals (and so the complex koshering laws of the Jews came into play...). And soon after that, God reveals a sort of *karma* that awaits those who slaughter animals: "By their own hands shall ye be slain." (*Genesis* 9:5)

WBAI: What happened next? Was meat-eating then at least "allowed" for all time?

SR: Well, not exactly, because there was a second attempt at instituting a vegetarian diet among the Jewish people. When the Israelites left Egypt, God provided "*manna*," a vegetarian substance, for food. Still even at that time, the people cried out for meat, and God indeed provided it—along with a plague for all who ate the meat.

They died immediately. The Bible makes careful record of this, and in no uncertain terms calls the burial places of those meat-eaters "the graves of lust." Biblical commentators—predisposed to vegetarianism or not—say that the graves were so named because those who were buried there had lusted after flesh foods.

WBAI: Steve, I'm just curious. What about "dominion?" Doesn't the Bible give man dominion over the animals?

SR: Indeed it does. But "dominion" was never taken to mean "abuser" or "exploiter." At least not according to traditional biblical usage. Rather, the original Hebrew for the word "dominion" is *yirdu*, and it connotes a sort of stewardship, or guardianship. In other words, we are given the command to "care for" our more humbly endowed brothers and sisters—the animals—not to eat them.

For instance, a king is said to have dominion over his subjects. But that doesn't mean that he should eat them, or abuse them. No. He must care for them, help them, and even love them.

I would also like to point out that this biblical verse which gives us dominion over the animals appears in *Genesis* 1:26. The verse recommending a vegetarian diet, which I have quoted earlier, appears in *Genesis* 1:29. Three verses later. In other words, God gives us dominion over the animals and, only three verses later, prohibits their use for food. Implicitly, the dominion he gives us cannot include using animals for food.

WBAI: That seems pretty clear. Why, I wonder, don't more religionists turn to vegetarianism? I mean it seems that there is a very strong case for it in the Bible. Maybe it's just arrogance or...

SR: Ignorance. Yes. There is evidence of both. In the Talmud, this arrogant side is explained quite a bit. It is summed up like this: "When man shall become proud in his heart," the Talmud tells us, "remind him that the little fly has preceded him in creation."

Also, the biblical book *Ecclesiastes* points out "For that which befalleth the sons of men, befalleth beasts, even one thing befalleth them: As the one dieth, so dieth the other. They have all one breath. So that a man hath no pre-eminence above a beast—for all is vanity." It's plain and simple fact: humans in general, especially in the twentieth century, have a perverse sort of prejudice toward the animals, one that is oftentimes unfounded.

Now let us deal with the question of ignorance. Rather than actually studying their scriptures and the ancient traditions from which these scriptures arose, many prefer to learn their religion by turning on the TV and watching Jim Baker and other popular evangelists. If people want to learn whether or not vegetarianism is actually consistent with their religion, they should make a serious study. Unfortunately, many are willing to accept whatever interpretation of their religion the majority accepts. One must develop the ability to distinguish a given spiritual path from those who claim to follow it.

WBAI: I agree totally. Steve, we've been focusing primarily on the Jewish tradition. I wonder if you could briefly discuss the Christian perspective.

SR: Basically, over the centuries, there has arisen two distinct schools of Christian thought: the Aristotelian-Thomistic school and the Augustinian-Franciscan school.

WBAI: Can you explain the difference and their relation to vegetarianism?

SR: Yes. The Aristotelian-Thomistic school has, as its fundamental basis, the premise that animals are here for our pleasure—they have no purpose of their own. We can eat them, torture them in laboratories—anything. This is almost Cartesian in scope. Unfortunately, modern Christianity embraces this form of their religion.

The Augustinian-Franciscan school, however, teaches that we are all brothers and sisters under God's fatherhood. Based largely on the world view of St. Frances and being platonic in nature, this school fits very neatly with the vegetarian perspective.

WBAI: Is there any evidence that Jesus was a vegetarian?

SR: Early Greek manuscripts speak of Jesus as "the Nazarene." I'll tell you why this is significant. Later editions of the Bible refer to "Jesus of Nazareth." And this simply means that he comes from that particular town: Nazareth. But research has revealed that this is a poor translation. A more accurate translation is "Jesus the Nazarene."

This is significant because it tells us more than merely the town he comes from, more than that he was just from Nazareth. It means he was from a sect called "the Nazarenes." And it is now known that this particular sect followed Essene principles, including vegetarianism.

WBAI: Do any modern Bibles translate it as "the Nazarene?"

SR: Yes. *The Jerusalem Bible* is one example. There are others. The point is this: he is definitely called "the Nazarene" in many places in the New Testament. So if you wanted to prove that he himself was a vegetarian, this would be a pretty convincing way to prove it. The Nazarenes were definitely vegetarians!

WBAI: Interesting. I was just reading in your book that many early Christian fathers were vegetarian. Historically, has this held true for many prominent Christians?

SR: *The Clementine Homilies*, which was written early in the second century and was based on the teachings of Saint Peter, Jesus's direct follower, categorically condemns all kinds of meat-eating and abuse of animals. Clement of Alexandria and even John Wesley, the founder of Methodism, were said to be vegetarians.

There is also a large body of literature devoted to proving that the original Apostles shunned the use of flesh foods, and one can read more about that in my book. The importance of establishing what the early Christians ate is considerable. It's crucial to my case, wouldn't you say?

WBAI: Definitely. It would indicate just what Christians today should eat. At least it would give an idea...

SR: That's right. In addition, it would give us more of an indication as to Jesus's dietary preferences.

WBAI: Right. Folks, I just want to urge you to go out and buy this book. It's just about the best book on the subject. *Food for the Spirit: Vegetarianism and the World Religions*, by author Steven Rosen. It also has a preface by Nobel laureate Isaac Baashevis Singer.

Steve, let's get into Eastern religion for a while. Vegetarianism, I know, is deeply ingrained in the Eastern way of thinking, especially in India. Isn't that true?

SR: Oh, definitely! In 1857, when the British introduced their new Enfield rifle to troops in Bengal, India, there was a great mutiny. Do you know why this occurred, this great, historic mutiny?

WBAI: No, why?

SR: Because that new Enfield rifle utilized an ammunition cartridge which was coated with animal grease. And the Sepoys, as those Bengali troops were called, had to bite off the tip of the cartridge before it was inserted in the rifle. Instead of conforming to this simple procedure, they mutinied. This is how deeply ingrained vegetarianism is in India.

WBAI: Where did this dedication to the meatless way of life begin? I know that the origins of Indian religion are shrouded in antiquity. But, still there must be some ancient practice or principle that India's modern day vegetarianism can be attributed to...

SR: Well, a lot of it has, as its fundamental basis, cow protection...

WBAI: Oh, yes, how did that come about?

SR: This can be attributed to the worship of Lord Krishna, who is always depicted as a cowherder. Although the Hindu pantheon is multi-faceted, originally, Krishna worship permeated the Vedic, or ancient Indian, tradition. And Krishna is glorified as being particularly fond of *brahmanas*, or those living beings who impart spiritual knowledge to others, and the cows, who give milk to one and all.

The cow is not worshipped in India, as is generally supposed. Rather, she is simply honored as "mother." Because she gives milk, as one's natural mother does. So for this reason, and because she is dear to Krishna—the Supreme Lord—she is, in a sense, revered. Or at least greatly respected.

WBAI: What about Mahatma Gandhi? Although he was a great, outspoken vegetarian, I had heard that he was inconsistent in many ways. Can you elaborate on that for a moment?

SR: I don't know if I, as a rule, would accuse Gandhi of inconsistency. After all, he was a deeply religious man and a devout vegetarian as well. Still, I have heard, probably, the same accusations to which you are referring. It has been said that Gandhi was a saint among politicians—but he was also a politician among the saints. Anyway, overall, I think he set a very good example of how one can be religious and a vegetarian at the same time.

WBAI: Since we don't have a lot of time left, maybe you could briefly explain to our WBAI listeners why the Eastern religions seem to be more conscious of the religious vegetarian imperative. Buddhism, Hinduism, Jainism—they all seem to immediately conjure up a religion of peace and harmlessness. Whereas the Judaeo-Christian tradition seems more shallow, at least in this particular area. Do you have anything to say about this?

SR: The eastern tradition promotes s*arva-bhuta-hita* ("devotion to the good of all creatures") over *loka-hita* ("devotion to the good of humanity"). The first ethical system, say the Vedas, includes the second, and is therefore more complete. If one cares for all living creatures, one naturally cares for humanity as well. The Vedic viewpoint states that one should see the same life-force in all living entities—regardless of "outer dress" (the body).

Those who cannot understand the principle of life in animals may then eventually misunderstand what the life-force is altogether and lose their sense of humanity. Accordingly, *sarva-bhuta-hita*, or the desire to do good for all creatures, is the superior code of ethics delineated in the Eastern religious traditions. It is, of course, the contention of *Food for the Spirit* that all of the major world religions acknowledged the superior, all-inclusive *sarva-bhuta-hita* at one time or another. Unfortunately, in the West especially, this truth has been adjusted, maligned, condemned and erased to suit the whims of political and religious figures across the centuries. We hope that our short book will right this wrong.

WBAI: Well, Steven, I want to sincerely thank you for coming on our show. And I want to say your presentation is certainly convincing in seeing vegetarianism as a religious imperative. Thank you again very much.

SR: Thank you.

(Previously published in *Animal Liberation Magazine* (October-December 1987), an Australian monthly.)

9

THE LIFE AND TIMES OF LORD CHAITANYA

FITNESS PLUS RADIO SHOW HOSTED BY ERICA ROBERTS (NEW YORK, JANUARY, 1990).

**P:** We have a special guest today—someone you may remember from before—the author Steven Rosen, or Satyaraja Dasa, as he's sometimes called. Last time we talked about Steve's book, *Food for the Spirit.* Today we're going to be talking about a different book Steve wrote called *India's Spiritual Renaissance: The Life and Times of Lord Chaitanya.* As I understand it, this book is actually going to be required reading at Yale's Department of Religious Studies, and Steve has also had the opportunity and, I suppose, pleasure of lecturing at Yale. Welcome to the show, Steve.

SR: Thank you.

FP: So, it's a provocative title: India's Spiritual Renaissance. What exactly *is* India's spiritual renaissance?

SR: India's spiritual renaissance *is* the life and times of Lord Chaitanya—literally. He revolutionized the Indian subcontinent in the late 15th and 16th centuries with His movement of *bhakti* or devotional love.

At that time, Europe was going through a renaissance as well. Western culture was moving toward a philosophy of humanism, moving more or less away from religion. It was a scientific age where we were beginning to discover the value of independent research divorced from any concept of God. So India at this time was moving in the opposite direction. The renaissance in India centered around the personality of Lord Chaitanya who, by the way, according to the ancient Vedic texts, is the most esoteric incarnation of God—the most important incarnation of all.

In India, He spearheaded a spiritual renaissance based on this doctrine of devotional love. He instigated social reform, religious reform—He brought back and expounded the original Vedic conception. And it all centered around the chanting of the holy name.

FP: That was kind of a bold claim you made about Lord Chaitanya's identity. How can this be substantiated historically from your perspective, the Vedic perspective. I mean there are many *avatars* and conceptions of God in India. Why, in your opinion, is Lord Chaitanya so special?

SR: That wasn't my opinion. That was a scriptural statement. There are many scriptural predictions about the appearance of Lord Chaitanya, proving His divinity. For example, *kalau sankirtanarambhe/ bhavisyami saci-sutah*. This is Sanskrit. That's a quote from the *Vayu Purana*, which predicts the appearance of Lord Chaitanya—that He'll come to inaugurate the sankirtan movement based on the chanting of the holy name. That particular verse even mentions His parentage: the son of Mother Sachi. And all these things did indeed come to be. So the predictions of the Vedic scriptures were realized in the person of Chaitanya Mahaprabhu and this is widely known throughout the Indian subcontinent.

FP: But it's His speciality that I'm trying to understand. Are there texts that point to His distinctive nature? You *did* say that He was the most important *avatar*—can you *prove* that, at least from within the framework of your tradition's scriptures?

SR: Oh, definitely! Kaviraj Goswami says it quite directly, in his *Chaitanya-charitamrita.* Actually, he declares that one cannot properly worship God—Radha and Krishna—without worshiping Chaitanya Mahaprabhu. He's quite adamant about it. And it is also emphasized by Prabodhananda Saraswati: "What benefit did the world attain when Lord Rama, Lord Nrisingha and many other incarnations of Godhead descended and killed the demons? How important is it that Lord Kapila revealed Sankhya philosophy and others revealed various systems of knowledge? Is it really so glorious that Brahma, Vishnu, and Shiva create, maintain, and destroy the material creation? Actually, we do not consider any of these things to be important compared to the descent of Shri Chaitanya Mahaprabhu. It is only by His grace that pure love of God—in its highest feature—is being distributed." It is there in the *Chaitanya-chandramrita,* chapter one. So He really brought the highest thing to this world. He created a renaissance even within a renaissance. Indian spirituality was already quite developed, but He took it even further...

FP: You keep mentioning the word "renaissance;" and indeed that's the title of your book. Why is Lord Chaitanya so important to India's spiritual reawakening.

SR: Yes, "reawakening" is actually a very good word. He didn't establish anything new, or anything that wasn't already embedded, at least confidentially, in the Vedic texts. He was reestablishing the ancient tradition of India which is *sanatan dharma* or the eternal function of the soul. This has a long history.

Sanatan dharma or the eternal function of the soul indicates that it's an eternal thing. So you can't say it has a beginning in history. But this Vedic knowledge was compiled by Vyasadeva about 5,000 years ago. Then in the course of time, about 2,500 years after the time of Vyasadeva, in the time of Lord Buddha, the Vedic teachings had become somewhat debased and Buddha...

FP: Could I interrupt? You said "debased." How so?

SR: At that time, the true tradition of *sanatan dharma* was becoming obscured and people were misinterpreting certain Vedic texts. For instance, the main reason Buddha appeared was to adjust the misapplied doctrine of making elaborate animal sacrifices—this was actually meant for a previous age. The priest would chant certain *mantras* and the animal that was killed would be rejuvenated in a new body. But there are no qualified priests in this age to do that, so the Vedas condemn such sacrifices in this age.

But the followers of the Vedic tradition at that time didn't know this. They were ill-informed and so Buddha came to enlighten them in this regard. In doing so, he rejected Vedic texts at this point and he said, "Just sit down and meditate. Don't kill the animals. Forget how you were interpreting the Vedas."

Then gradually in the eighth century, Shankaracharya appeared and he reestablished the Vedic texts. But because he was preaching to Buddhists he had to teach a sort of impersonalist view of the Vedic texts.

He couldn't give the full doctrine of personalism as Vyasa had done. But he was successful in reestablishing the Vedic texts and he drove Buddhism out of India to the neighboring countries. Then after Shankaracharya appeared, Ramanujacharya appeared in the 10th century and brought it even further than Shankaracharya with his philosophy which was technically known as *vishishtadvaita*. This was a sort of qualified monism. Ramanuja gave a little bit more information, showing that we are not exactly one with God as Shankara had taught. He said that we're also different from God.

And this philosophy was brought even further in the 13th century by Madhvacharya. His philosophy was known as *dvaita*. We are definitely distinct from God. We are not the same as God. This was the crux of Madhva's teaching, couched, of course, in complex theological terms.

Finally, Chaitanya Mahaprabhu appeared in the 16th century and He completely reestablished (hence, this word *renaissance)* the original Vedic conclusion by contributing His philosophy of *achintya-bhedabheda tattva*, which means that inconceivably the living entity is simultaneously one with God in quality and different from God in quantity.

In other words, God is all-knowing, and we have some knowledge; God is all-attractive, we have some attractive features; God is omnipresent, but we're present in one place at a time. So we are qualitatively similar to God, but He is far greater than we are. Chaitanya Mahaprabhu and His followers explained these things in minute detail. In that way, they reestablished the original Vedic *sanatan dharma* system.

FP: It's really fascinating and certainly very deep. You seem to be implying that there's a method to this madness, so to speak. There seems to be a definite chronology or sort of purpose or progression from one *avatar* to the next, or one teacher to another. Am I right?

SR: Yes.

FP: I guess there's not much more we can say about that. I was just wondering: is there any comparison between Lord Chaitanya and Jesus Christ, for example. Are there any parallels which can be drawn?

SR: There are many parallels. Some have called Lord Chaitanya the Jesus Christ of India, in fact. He performed miracles like Jesus Christ. He would raise certain people from the dead. Shrivasa Thakur was one of His intimate associates. He raised his son from the dead. On another occasion, when His followers were hungry, He put a mango seed in the ground and a tree immediately grew and gave more mangos than His followers could eat. Miracles similar to the ones ascribed to Jesus Christ are also ascribed to Lord Chaitanya.

There are also similarities in His doctrine, which is basically a doctrine of love. Jesus Christ taught to love and honor God with your heart, mind and soul, and Lord Chaitanya's emphasis on *bhakti*, or devotional love, was the exact same principle. Also Jesus taught, "Our Father who art in Heaven, hallowed be Thy name," or "He who calls upon the name of the Lord shall be saved." These statements are there in biblical literature. Lord Chaitanya also emphasized the chanting of the holy name, though He emphasized it in great detail. He taught especially the chanting of the *maha-mantra*: *Hare Krishna, Hare Krishna, Krishna Krishna, Hare Hare/ Hare Rama, Hare Rama, Rama Rama, Hare Hare*, which is basically a very pure prayer. It doesn't ask anything of the Lord. It simply asks: "O my Lord, O energy of the Lord, please engage me in Your service." Lord Chaitanya came to teach this kind of unmotivated, unconditional love.

FP: I just want to backtrack a little bit. In the comparisons between Jesus Christ and Lord Chaitanya, you repeatedly use the word "*avatar.*" Maybe you could define for us what the word "avatar" really means. That's a word everyone has heard but, I don't think, anyone really understands.

SR: When Lord Chaitanya did a tour of South India, just prior to that, He went to Benares and met with His intimate follower Sanatan Goswami. When He was there He gave a complete detailed explanation of the *avatar* system and how God descends. *Avatar* literally means "the descent of God." Lord Chaitanya is known in the Vedic tradition as an *avatari*, which means "the source of all incarnations." But He explained to Sanatan Goswami all the details of this "incarnation phenomenon," if you will.

I'll give you a brief overview: Krishna is a name for the original Personality of Godhead. That identity of God is called *svayam rupa*. *Svayam rupa* can break down into His energies or His immediate expansions. His immediate expansions are known as *tad-ekatma rupa* and they can further expand into *shaktyavesh avatars*. Jesus Christ would fit neatly into the category of *shaktyavesh avatar*, which literally means "an empowered entity who works on behalf of God for a particular purpose." He appears in a particular time, place and circumstance for a specific purpose in enlightening people about God consciousness.

FP: Would Buddha fall into that category also?

SR: Yes. Exactly.

FP: There are different kinds of *avatars*, then, and they have different functions, they have different potencies, etc. Wow! My head is swimming. [Laughter] This is fascinating. Is there anything else unique about Lord Chaitanya, anything else that He's contributed?

What is the goal of this whole thing for the individual? What significance does this whole movement that He started have? You mentioned the *mantra* before—the one that He emphasized? That's the one we hear the Hare Krishnas chant, too. I would like you to talk more about that. But first, can you tell us something about the ultimate goal? Can you elaborate?

SR: The goal is to develop love for God. Lord Chaitanya broke it down into a detailed science for His followers. Previous to Lord Chaitanya, they had elucidated upon the primary types of relationships one might have with the Lord as a servant, or as a son, or one may have a relationship in the parental mood, or as a friend; but Lord Chaitanya's special contribution was the *madhurya rasa*, the *rasa* of divine love, the relationship of conjugal affection. But this is transcendental—spiritual—and it is never to be confused with its mundane counterpart. Such a conjugal *rasa* is rarely achieved, but it *is* considered the highest.

FP: So you're actually saying we could have a very intimate loving relationship with God.

SR: But it's divorced from the unsavory characteristics of love relationships in this world. One shouldn't mistake it for the carnal love that one experiences in the material world. It is the original spiritual counterpart of that. Just as that is the highest kind of excitement in this world, the spiritual counterpart is also the highest kind of relationship one might have with God.

FP: I'm sure this sounds very esoteric and a little difficult to grasp for many who might be listening to the show, and . . .

SR: Wait, let me tell you something really interesting about Lord Chaitanya. There are two primary reasons for this descent, one is external and exoteric and the other is internal or esoteric. The external reason for Lord Chaitanya's descent as I said before was simply to inaugurate the *sankirtan* movement, to establish the chanting of the holy name as the means for God-realization in this age.

But the internal reason for His appearance is very special. Even though God has infinite wisdom, He desires to taste the love that His devotees feel for Him. Now this love is also infinite and is best expressed in the mood of Shrimati Radharani.

FP: Now, who is She, pray tell?

SR: Shrimati Radharani is the female counterpart of the male Absolute Personality of Godhead. In the Vedic system, God is not just male, He's male and female.

FP: I'm sure all our feminists out there will be very glad to hear that.

SR: Yes. Absolutely. That's right. So Radharani's love for Krishna is the essence of a pure devotee's love for Krishna and so to experience that love, the Lord descends as Chaitanya Mahaprabhu. Radha and Krishna both descend in that form. Krishna is doing this primarily so He can experience Radharani's love for Him. This is a highly esoteric concept.

It may be asked, "Why, if God is all-knowing, does He have to descend as Chaitanya Mahaprabhu in some extraneous way to understand the love that His pure devotees feel for Him?" And the answer is that Lord Chaitanya is *not* extraneous to God's self-existent nature. It is simply giving the *methodology* of how God understands His pure devotees' love for Him. The methodology—the *how*—is the form of Chaitanya Mahaprabhu.

FP: So what you're saying—to bring it down to earth a little bit—is that Lord Chaitanya is playing a part, so to speak?

SR: Yes, He's playing the role of a devotee. He is God Himself in the form of a devotee—this is the orthodox Vaishnava tradition.

It is very significant because usually when God descends, He shows His unlimited pastimes. He performs extraordinary activities—not to say that Lord Chaitanya didn't—but He also set the perfect example of how a devotee should behave in his day-to-day life.

FP: Let me stop you right there. What exactly is a devotee?

SR: A devotee of Krishna is one who offers whatever he does, whatever he gets or gives to others—he does everything as a sacrament to the Lord. That definition is traceable to the teachings in the *Bhagavad-gita*, which is part of the Vedic literature that I've been mentioning throughout the show.

A devotee is someone who is devoted. [Laughter] There are many accepted definitions, even according to the Vedic literature. On the one side, it has a very strict definition—one must be totally given to the Lord's service. On the other hand, there are very liberal definitions. Lord Chaitanya said that even one who merely appreciates the holy name—he can be counted amongst the devotees. An even broader definition includes all living beings, since ontologically all souls are constitutionally servants of Krishna.

FP: I can understand that. But the more demanding definitions—that sounds like an awfully high standard. Just to someone who is listening to the show and to myself, it sounds very complex, it sounds like there are a lot of requirements. Is the process very difficult?

SR: No, no. It is a very simple process and it centers on chanting the holy name of the Lord. That's all. That's the basis. That's the heart of the process. And by chanting the holy name of the Lord, which is considered non-different from the Lord, since the Lord is absolute, one can achieve perfection in this process. But we're talking about the ultimate reality here, so obviously on the higher levels it does require a great amount of commitment. There are many rules and regulations. But, in the beginning, one can simply chant the holy name. From that, everything else will come.

On the very rudimentary level, for instance, in the very beginning there's *anda-bhishbas*. *Anda-bhishbhas* means "blind faith," and most religionists in the world are still on this level. That's at the very beginning of any process whether it is an atheistic life or a spiritualist's life. He has blind faith initially until he gathers some experiential knowledge. Then he graduates to the level of *shraddha* or faith that is more grounded in something real. *Shraddha* is actually considered the first real level of perfection in *bhakti-yoga.*

There are nine levels of perfection. From *shraddha* one can graduate to the level of *sadhu-sanga.* In other words if you have that firm faith, you want to associate with other persons who also have that firm faith. From there you reach the level of *bhajana-kriya*, which means you take initiation from a pure devotee of the Lord and develop your meditational abilities. From there, *anartha-nivritti*, you start to unburden yourself of unwanted bad habits. It just goes on and on until you reach the levels of *bhava* and *prema*, which is like unconditional love of God, and that is a very complex level. But initially the process centers around chanting the holy name, and Lord Chaitanya said that there are no hard and fast rules for chanting these names.

FP: So I'll pull back down again a little bit and ask you what exactly are the benefits of chanting. Like you've just been describing what seems to be a whole progression of spiritual reawakening? Is this all to be derived from the chanting? I mean, is chanting really that potent?

SR: Oh yes, chanting is at the heart of spiritual life. All religious traditions recommend to chant the name of God. Jesus even said, "Where few are gathered together in my name, I am there." That is because the name is absolute. Just like in this world, Erica the name and Erica the person are two different things. But in the spiritual world, which is the exact opposite of the material world, the exact opposite must be true. A person and his name must be non-different—if in this world a person and his name are different. So that's the absolute nature of Krishna and His name. So if you associate with God either directly or through chanting His name, you're going to become purified. Purification ultimately brings you to the level of love of God and that's the goal.

And as I said before the Hare Krishna *maha-mantra* that Lord Chaitanya recommended is a very pure prayer. It asks God for nothing, not "give us our daily bread" or anything of the kind. It simply says, "I don't care what You give me, but I want to engage in Your pure unalloyed service." Such a pure prayer naturally brings a person to a very exalted state of consciousness in due course.

FP: So, as it were, we become completely unconcerned or divorced from this material or physical existence.

SR: No, not at all. But we learn the proper utility of this physical existence. Everything is coming from God and therefore everything is meant to be used in God's service. It's not like dry renunciants sometimes teach, "Just give up the material world." That's not Lord Chaitanya's teaching. His teaching is that we use everything in the service of God. There's a proper utilization for everything, and that's what *bhakti-yoga* teaches.

FP: So it's conceivable that I could have an ordinary job, etc., and still apply this process. I don't have to be living on a mountaintop to do this.

SR: Oh, absolutely not. Just see. We're doing this radio show. We're using microphones and headphones and all kinds of complex equipment, but we're using them in God's service.

FP: I see. Well, I want the listening audience to know that I *did* read this book, or at least a very considerable portion of it, and one thing I did notice, Steve, is that you kept mentioning an individual named Prabhupada as your spiritual master. And I was wondering what is his significance to this movement or this chanting to the rest of the world?

SR: Well, you know it's interesting that Lord Chaitanya predicted five hundred years ago when He appeared in India that in every town and village of the world, that the holy name of Krishna will be chanted. At the time, and for hundreds of years after, this seemed like a very revolutionary statement. But Prabhupada is the one who brought this prediction to reality. He took the name of Krishna out of India and spread it to every town and village of the world.

And it's an interesting thing that in 1896, a great spiritual master named Bhaktivinode Thakur wrote a book on Lord Chaitanya and sent it to the West, and that was the very first time Lord Chaitanya's teachings were given in the English language. But get this: two weeks after that, Prabhupada was born and he's the one who actually took the Vedic culture to the Western countries.

FP: Did Prabhupada know Bhaktivinode Thakur? Was he a personality with whom he was acquainted?

SR: Very much acquainted. Not physically acquainted, but they belong to the same preceptorial line of disciplic succession. That line began with Krishna Himself and there were many personalities in that line. Lord Chaitanya Himself adhered to that line. As I said, He was setting the example of a perfect devotee. Therefore, he aligned Himself with this disciplic line technically known as the Brahma-Madhva-Gaudiya sampradaya. It is called Gaudiya because Lord Chaitanya was from Bengal, also known as Gauda-desh, and He personally revitalized this line.

FP: So Prabhupada actually seems to be a historical figure within a very long chain of spiritual teachers.

SR: Correct. Sometime after Lord Chaitanya, this Bhaktivinode Thakur was in the line, and Bhaktivinode Thakur's son, Bhaktisiddhanta Sarasvati Thakur is also in that line, and Prabhupada was a disciple of Bhaktisiddhanta Sarasvati Thakur. So there's that intimate link.

FP: Speaking of intimate links, the philosophy is very interesting. But I'm wondering if there any many people linked to it today. Who is actually practicing this today?

SR: Oh, in India, especially, there are so many people that are related to the Gaudiya Vaishnava sampradaya. Millions. In the West, I'm sure everyone is familiar with the devotees of the Hare Krishna movement, the International Society for Krishna Consciousness. When you see them on the street corners chanting Hare Krishna, don't think that they are some saffron-clad weirdos. They actually represent an age-old tradition beginning with Krishna Himself. They properly represent Chaitanya Mahaprabhu's lineage.

FP: So someone just going on externals, I guess, would be surprised to learn that there's a great deal of depth and tradition to it all. I often see them when I'm passing through the train station at Times Square.

SR: Well, people who go on externals are going to be misled about a great number of things in life.

FP: Is there anything you'd like to add in the few minutes we have left?

SR: Well, there are eight prayers attributed to Lord Chaitanya Himself and I think they best embody His teachings of chanting the holy name. I would like to at least recite one or two of them.

He says, "Let there be all victory for the chanting of the holy name of Krishna, which can cleanse the mirror of the heart and stop the miseries of the blazing fire of material existence. That chanting is the waxing moon that spreads the lotus of good fortune for all living entities. It is the life and soul of all education. The chanting of the holy name of Krishna expands the blissful ocean of transcendental life. It gives a cooling effect to everyone and it enables one to taste full nectar at every step."

There's another verse that Lord Chaitanya gave in which you get a feeling for the catholic nature of His teaching—the nonsectarian nature— because He says that not just the name Krishna can be used, but any genuine name of God. He says: "O my Lord, O Supreme Personality of Godhead, in Your holy name there is all good fortune for the living entity and, therefore, You have unlimited names such as 'Krishna' and 'Govinda' by which You expand Yourself. You have invested all Your potencies in these names and there are no hard and fast rules for remembering them or chanting them. My Lord, although you bestow such mercy upon the fallen conditioned souls by liberally teaching Your holy names, I am so unfortunate that I commit offenses while chanting the holy name and therefore I do not achieve attachment for chanting."

This is the humility and the teaching of the holy name.

FP: Just listening to it sounds as though its universal in scope. It does seem to come through: the nonsectarianism of it.

SR: That wasn't emphasized only by Lord Chaitanya but by all of His followers since—even the Hare Krishna movement today emphasizes the nonsectarian universal chanting of the holy name. Whatever your religious tradition, get in touch with God by chanting His holy names. That's the message of Lord Chaitanya's teaching.

FP: Well it *has* been mind-boggling [Laughter], if also enlightening. Really, it is a fascinating subject. We've been talking with Steven Rosen, author of *India's Spiritual Renaissance: The Life and Times of Lord Chaitanya*. Where can we get the book, Steve?

SR: You can get the book at East-West Books, Samuel Weiser's. It is also available at every Hare Krishna temple in the country.

FP: Thank you very much.

(Previously published as a booklet in 1990.)

SHIKSHASHTAKAM:
THE EIGHT PRAYERS
OF LORD CHAITANYA

A SERIES OF TALKS AT THE NEW YORK PUBLIC LIBRARY

INTRODUCTORY ADDRESS: August 8, 1990

I would first of all like to thank Dr. Lundquist and the librarians affiliated with the Oriental Division for allowing us to meet and discuss this particular aspect of Oriental philosophy. Although we've had some informal discussions in the past, we can now more methodically pursue the philosophy of Shri Chaitanya, especially in regard to His eight verses. These important *shlokas*, as they are called, contain the sum and substance of Indian religious thought and indeed of all spiritual philosophy.

Some background information is in order. Shri Chaitanya Mahaprabhu was a pre-eminent religious figure of the sixteenth century who, for some reason, remains quite unknown today, especially in the West. Even in India, though, His true position is often concealed—His glory is not generally known. One possible explanation for His curious lack of popularity may be traced to His minimal literary activity. Like

Jesus and Buddha before Him, Mahaprabhu left no literary contribution to speak of. His eight original prayers, which we will be discussing at length, *are* considered original compositions, although they were not written down in the usual sense. They were profound devotional outpourings, which He sang in an enhanced state of spiritual ecstasy. These were eventually written down by Mahaprabhu's intimate follower, Shri Swarup Damodar.

Of course, Mahaprabhu instructed His intimate disciples, chief amongst whom were the Six Goswamis of Vrindavan, to elaborately delineate, in a scholarly way, His message of scientific devotion, His message of advanced spirituality, His message of love of God. This they did—in great detail—and Mahaprabhu's teachings later came to be known as the philosophy of Gaudiya Vaishnavism. So although Mahaprabhu Himself left little in the way of written documents, His followers left a vast wealth of philosophical literature, codifying and systematizing Mahaprabhu's teachings for future generations.

Aside from Chaitanya Mahaprabhu's negligible literary career, another, more important reason for His concealed or confidential mission lay in the fact that He was a particularly esoteric manifestation, an *avatar*—the *Golden* avatar, as He is sometimes called—and this is why He really remains unknown. He is the *channa* avatar, or the hidden Incarnation of God.

You see, God's many appearances in this world are predicted in ancient India's Vedic literature, the world's most time-honored and comprehensive scriptural tradition. In these ancient Vedic texts, the general descent of God is described, and it is usually quite specific, referring to His parentage, the town in which He makes His appearance, the mission He seeks to accomplish, and things of this nature. It is very scientific. So there can be no mistake about an Incarnation's authenticity.

In recent years, especially since the '60s, it has become fashionable to sentimentally accept someone as a *guru* or, worse still, to accept them as an Incarnation of God, based on whimsy, speculation, or gut impressions. But this is very risky. Cheaters abound. It is sometimes difficult to separate the saints from the swindlers, the *avatars* from the avaricious. For this reason, Shri Sanatan Goswami, a direct disciple of Chaitanya Mahaprabhu, asked his Master, "*kemane janiba kalite kon avatar?*" This is the Bengali. It means, "How can I

understand who is the Incarnation of God for this current age of Kali?"
And so Mahaprabhu answered him, "One can understand that someone
is an Incarnation in this age in the exact same way that he could have
ascertained such a thing in previous ages: By consulting the scriptures."
This is the secret.

The scriptures reveal exact information—specific things to look
for in an alleged Incarnation. First, there is *swarup-lakshana*. This refers
to personal characteristics, such as bodily features, nature, and form—
external things that one can observe. Then there is *tatastha-lakshana*.
This refers to marginal characteristics, such as specific information
about His transcendental activities. In other words, there is a reason
why an Incarnation descends—and it's not just to collect money, grow
a long beard, and to look holy on special holidays! So one who learns
this transcendental science from a teacher in disciplic succession—a
teacher who represents one of the four genuine Vaishnava
sampradayas and who does not deviate from the information
delineated in the scriptures—such a person will not be cheated. There
is thus a way to objectively distinguish the genuine Incarnation from a
bogus person.

Chaitanya Mahaprabhu was specifically described in the
scriptures and so according to these standards He is rightly accepted as
an Incarnation of the Supreme. But let's backtrack for a second. The
scriptures describe many different Incarnations in great detail. For
example, Buddha is predicted, and the names of His parents and village
are specifically mentioned. So, too, are a host of other avatars
mentioned, or predicted, in this same exacting way.

Some are explained in a general way, but not so general that it
is left vague. Rupa Goswami's *Laghu-bhagavatamrita*, for example,
says that the Lord appears in Satya-yuga, with a white complexion, and
He is known as Shukla. In the next age, Treta-yuga, He appears as
Rakta or Makhamuk, the avatar with a red complexion. In the following
age, known as Dvapara-yuga, He comes as Shyam and He has a blue or
darkish complexion. Finally, in Kali, the present age, He comes in a
Blackish form and is thus known as Krishna. Sometimes, though, it is
described that in Dvapara-yuga He has a yellowish complexion and in
Kali He comes as Shyam. Be that as it may, this is the general course of
events as the *yuga* cycles rotate for millions and billions of years.

But, still, in esoteric parts of the Vedic literature, there is
mentioned a rare *golden* avatar—or one with a yellowish complexion—

one who rarely appears. A secret, esoteric Incarnation. The eleventh canto of the *Bhagavatam*, for instance, tells us that in a rare Kali-yuga, which occurs only in the twenty-eighth divya-yuga of the seventh Manvantar—that is to say: it occurs every 8,664,000,000 years, or something like that—this special Golden Avatar appears. This is Chaitanya Mahaprabhu. Therefore, in this special point in our evolution of yuga cycles, the Lord is called "Tri-yuga," or "He who only appears in three of the four ages." Why? Because in the fourth age He is *channa* Avatar, or the special, hidden Incarnation.

So in the current configuration of yugas, the Lord descends as a white Incarnation in Satya-yuga, as previously, a red Incarnation in Treta-yuga, as previously, and a darkish Incarnation in Dvapara-yuga, as previously (with the one exception that this time it is not an ordinary darkish avatar but the original personality of Godhead Himself, Krishna). But this time, also, in this particular Kali-yuga, the Lord descends in a special golden complexion. The original, supreme personality of Godhead descends for a special mission. This is the glory of Shri Chaitanya Mahaprabhu, and was confirmed in the *Shrimad Bhagavatam* and in other scriptures as well.

Question: You are referring to the predictions in the Vedic texts?

Satyaraja Dasa: Oh, yes. There is much more concrete evidence for the divinity of Mahaprabhu Specific scriptural predictions, with reference to *swarup-lakshana* and *tatastha-lakshana* (those two types of evidences that I just mentioned)—these are abundantly found throughout Vedic texts. For example, there are direct statements in the *Mahabharata*, the *Bhagavatam*, and there is even a book known as *Chaitanya Upanishad* which is supposedly appended to the *Atharva Veda*. The *Krishna-yamala* and the *Brahma-yamala* both specifically mention His mother Sachi's name and the town of Navadvip, where He took His birth, and these two scriptures also specifically mention His mission: the sankirtan movement, or the movement that centers around the congregational chanting of the holy name.

The *Vayu Purana* also says: *Kalau sankirtanarambhe bhavishyami sachi sutaha*, or "In the age of Kali when the Sankirtan movement is inaugurated, Krishna will descend as the divine son of Sachidevi." So Chaitanya Mahaprabhu's divinity is fully acknowledged in the Vedic literature, and scholars of the Gaudiya Vaishnava tradition have brought this out in many academic works and lucid writings. Especially in the writings of His Divine Grace A. C. Bhaktivedanta

Swami Prabhupada—if one carefully reads his translation and commentary of *Chaitanya-charitamrita*, one will be convinced of the pre-eminent position of Lord Chaitanya.

Question: But in India, at least, Shri Chaitanya is not recognized by everyone. If He were such an important avatar, as you indicate, then you would imagine that He would be accepted across the board.

Satyaraja Dasa: [laughter] In this age, *nothing* is accepted across the board. This is the age of disharmony and argumentation. [laughter] Actually, what you are bringing out is the real glory, or the inner meaning, of *channa* avatar. Mahaprabhu's mission is confidential—the most secret of all secrets. Therefore, the *Bhagavatam* predicts that only the most intelligent will recognize His glory: "In the age of Kali the Lord incarnates as a devotee, yellowish in color, and is always chanting the holy name—*Hare Krishna, Hare Krishna, Krishna Krishna, Hare Hare/ Hare Rama, Hare Rama, Rama Rama, Hare Hare.* Although He is Krishna, His complexion is not blackish like Krishna's, but it is golden. He preaches love of God through His sankirtan movement, and those living entities who have sufficient brain substance, or who are sufficiently intelligent (*yajanti hi sumedhasaha*)—they will adopt His method of realization." (S.B. 11.5.32)

So this is the great secret of the scriptures. It is no wonder that it is accepted by a fortunate few! But Krishna had warned that it would be so. In His *Gita*, He says that "out of many millions of people, only a handful will look for perfection. And out of that handful, hardly one will know Me in truth." (B.G. 7:3) So this can be said to directly relate to Chaitanya Mahaprabhu. Only a rare breed will take it up. Those who are serious. Those who want love of God and nothing else.

"What?!" you may ask incredulously. "You are making an exclusive group for Chaitanya followers?! A rare and serious breed indeed!" No. It is not an ego game. The exalted stature of Mahaprabhu's devotees should not be taken as a pompous sentiment. It is open to everyone. Simply chant the holy name! Whatever your religion. Whatever your language. Chant God's name and devote your life to His glorification. If you do this much then you are a practitioner of Mahaprabhu's method, at least in a fundamental sense. So it is not exclusive. We don't say that one must become a Hindu, or Jew, or Christian, or anything. No. Just develop love for God. This is the actual substance of Mahaprabhu's nonsectarian message, and it can be embraced by everyone.

What is the result? The highest realization. Our Mahaprabhu is not only Krishna, but Radha and Krishna combined. Therefore Vaishnavas sing, *shri Krishna Chaitanya Radha-Krishna nahe anya*: "Radha and Krishna combined together are Shri Chaitanya Mahaprabhu." Swarup Damodar has sung like this. Full manifestation. Male and Female Absolute. Radha and Krishna. The most complete manifestation of Godhead. This is the verdict of the Gaudiya *sampradaya*. So, in answer to your question, yes, it is a rare thing—not widely accepted. But that is not very shocking. If you have a rare gem, you should not expect that everyone will have what it takes to purchase it...

Question: I am curious about documentation. How accurate are the stories relating to Shri Chaitanya's life? Were biographies written much later, or were they written during His own time period?

Satyaraja Dasa: Oh. It is well known. You may find it interesting that more than any other religious figure, perhaps, Mahaprabhu was written about in His own lifetime, and shortly thereafter. *Chaitanya-charita*, a lengthy work by Kavi Karnapur, one of Lord Chaitanya's con-temporaries, and Karnapur's *Chaitanya Chandrodoy-natakam* also—these were the early biographies. And then there were the diaries kept by Murari Gupta...and one by Swarup Damodar, and one by Raghunath Das Goswami...and Mahaprabhu's personal servant's diary. Right. Govinda's diary...so....And Vrindavan Das Thakur's *Chaitanya Bhagavat*. This was the most authoritative....and two others—Krishna Das Kaviraj Goswami's *Chaitanya-charitamrita* and Lochan Das Thakur's *Chaitanya Mangal*—these are the most authoritative biographies, written a generation or two after Mahaprabhu's disappearance. Great scholarly works. And then there is Chudamani Das's *Gauranga-vijoy* and the *Gaur-pada-tarangini*. And the *Gauranga-champu*...

Oh...there is no limit! You see, He was known as a divinity in His own time. So contemporaries and devotees of the following two generations took it upon themselves to write many books in order to capture the pastimes. His history, the sequence of events—it is well documented. I've also written a book based on these authoritative sources—a book about Mahaprabhu's historical biography...the sequence of events. In my work, I have also made prodigious use of our Shrila Prabhupada's writings and the writings of Bhaktivinode Thakur, who has given many specific details about the historicity and divinity of Lord Chaitanya's pastimes. So this is my special field...

Question: I would certainly not debate His divinity, or even His special position among *avatars*. That is an in-house question. I think that there are many Vaishnavas in India—thousands if not millions—who accept Krishna as God Almightly, and many of these people accept Chaitanya as well. And certainly in the West He is becoming very well-known through the endeavors of the Hare Krishna movement. But I'm more curious about Chaitanya as an historical personality. Can you give us an outline of His life, at least those parts that are accepted by academicians? Just the facts. Not the dogma. Not the whole thing. Of course, it may be difficult to separate fact from fiction. Maybe...if you could give just a brief synopsis....You see, I just want to put Him in historical perspective. I'm not sure if dates are attributable...

Satyaraja Dasa: I'm just going to briefly mention the important dates in His manifest pastimes, as you've requested. Just so you can get an idea. For details you can read the xerox copies I've made for you. And then we will discuss His eight original prayers. Perhaps a brief life summary will give greater insight into these prayers. But where to begin?...

Question: Was Shri Chaitanya his full name?

Satyaraja Dasa: He was initially known as Vishvambar Mishra, at birth, and later He was known as Nimai Pandit, and still later (after becoming a renunciant) as Chaitanya Mahaprabhu. He was born on Friday, February 18, 1486, at least by Western reckoning. His birth took place in Navadvip, also known as Mayapur, West Bengal.

Navadvip, at that time, was in a terrible condition. Although it was the seat of Sanskrit learning—a well-known University town—it was giving way to sinful life. Cheaters and cheated. That's all. Haridas Thakur and Advaita Acharya, two great saints from the local area, prayed for Lord Chaitanya's descent. Consequently, in answer to their prayers, He came to inaugurate His sankirtan movement—this was His external reason for coming. The internal reason is theologically elaborate. Suffice it to say that in the descent of Chaitanya Mahaprabhu, God tastes the love of His topmost devotees. This love is so intense that God wishes to directly experience it from their unique perspective. So He appears in this world as His own perfect devotee—as Chaitanya Mahaprabhu—in order to fully taste this divine love, the most cherished goal.

But let us go on. The Summer that followed His winter birth, in 1486, was a happy one for his parents, Jagannath Mishra and Sachidevi. That August they performed the traditional Hindu grain ceremony, where their child ate His first grains, and then they performed another traditional ceremony wherein money, foodstuffs and holy scriptures are placed before the child. By seeing which item the youth spontaneously grabs for, they are able to predict His future inclinations. Young Mahaprabhu, then known as little Nimai, reached for the *Shrimad Bhagavatam*, religious scripture par excellence.

In approximately 1494, when He was about eight years of age, He began school under the tutelage of Ganga Das Pandit. Two years later, in 1496, when He was ten, He became known as a great scholar, having mastered several languages, logic, rhetoric, hermeneutics, and philosophy. It was in this year, too, that His elder brother, Vishvarup, took *sannyasa*, or the renounced order of life, and became a traveling mendicant. He would never again see Vishvarup, although some say that Vishvarup came back to Him in the form of Nityananda Prabhu, His intimate associate. It is also said that when Mahaprabhu first put on His sacred thread, He also felt reunited with Vishvarup, since Balaram (a.k.a. Vishvarup) incarnates as the Lord's paraphernalia, such as His sacred thread. Anyway, Vishvarup's vow of *sannyasa* and His concomitant leaving home had had a deep influence on little Nimai.

Four years later, in the year 1500, He took Lakshmipriya as His wife. He was fourteen years old. This is not uncommon in India—an arranged marriage at an early age. The couple grow up together and develop a very deep love and affection—it is not merely based on physical attraction and overplayed romantic fantasies, as it often is in the West. Of course, it needs to be understood that the Lord's marriage is not ordinary. Theologically, this is the principle of *Shri*, *Bhu*, and *Neela*. In other words, when the Lord descends to the earthly realm, He descends with His eternal associates. Chaitanya Mahaprabhu's wife, Lakshmipriya, is a manifestation of *Shri-shakti*, the Lord's internal energy. Another manifestation of this energy is *Bhu-shakti*, and She descends as the Lord's second wife, Shrimati Vishnu-priya, whom we shall soon mention. The word *Neela* refers to the particular place of pastimes—in this case it refers to Mayapur or Navadvip-dham.

Anyway, in 1502, now sixteen years old and happily married, He opened His own *tol* ("school") and began teaching grammar. It was during this period, in fact, that He wrote His own commentary on an intricate Sanskrit grammar, which, regretably, is no longer extant. All things considered, this could have been a very fulfilling and prosperous time. However, the biographical historians inform us that this general period was full of calamities.

While Mahaprabhu was away in His ancestral village, deep in East Bengal, which is now known as Bangladesh, His wife died when She was bitten by a poisonous snake. The reverential biographers say that it was the poisonous snake of separation that took Her life. It is said that at His mother's request, He quickly remarried. The new bride was Vishnupriya, the manifestation of *Bhu-shakti*, who was to become one of the most important female models in the Gaudiya Vaishnava community.

Lord Chaitanya's father left this mortal world that same year, and so later that year, or perhaps early the next year, in 1503, the Lord traveled to Gaya, in Bihar province, to perform the funeral rites for His departed father. There, in Gaya, He met Ishvara Puri, a great saint who He had seen once before in Mayapur, and there He took initiation from Ishwara Puri into the chanting of the holy name. Thus, when Mahaprabhu was about seventeen years of age, He was given the ten-syllable Gopal mantra, a confidential incantation which translates into something like "Salutations to the beloved of the gopis." The gopis, as you know, are the transcendental loving cowherd maidens—Krishna's greatest devotees.

Along with this *mantra*, Lord Chaitanya was given the Hare Krishna *maha-mantra*, which you know: *Hare Krishna, Hare Krishna, Krishna Krishna, Hare Hare/ Hare Rama, Hare Rama, Rama Rama, Hare Hare.* This means, "O Lord! O Energy of the Lord! Please engage me in Your causeless service." And He also chanted *Hari haraye nama krishna yadavaya namaha*—a song made up of various names for Lord Krishna. These are the two great Krishna *mantras*—along with the Gopal mantra—and by chanting these under the direction of a bona-fide spiritual master—in His case, Ishvara Puri—He soon became God-intoxicated. This is the secret. We must receive our *mantra* in disciplic succession. If we do, then a vital transformation can take place, as it did in the life of Nimai Pandit—divine love started to emanate from His very being. The Pandit gave way to Prema. Dialectics moved aside and Devotion reigned supreme.

Anyway, let's continue. For the next six years, the transformed Nimai, Chaitanya Mahaprabhu, was like a live wire, surcharging everyone with pure love of Godhead. Now twenty-three years old, He had long since closed His school so He could devote full time to His religion of love. He organised a massive sankirtan movement centered around the congregational chanting. Rogues, such as Jagai and Madhai, became superlative devotees. The most erudite scholars, like Keshava Kashmiri, were eventually humbled by Lord Chaitanya. Even powerful political leaders in the Islamic government, such as Chand Kazi, were soon overtaken by the current of divine love. All of Mayapur was inundated with the glories of the holy name.

Then, when He was twenty-four, in the beginning of 1510, He travelled to nearby Katwa and was initiated into the renounced order of life by Keshava Bharati. The devotees did not like seeing Him adopt the renounced life of a mendicant. Their love for Him was quite intense, beyond words, and so with great dread they contemplated the fact that He would have to perform severe austerities. Madhu, the barber who was to cut His beautiful locks of hair, wept pitifully as he did his duty. The others, Prabhu Nityananda, Acharyaratna, and Mukunda Datta— others were there as well—watched everything transpire in disbelief. Nonetheless, to set the proper example and to win the respect of the religious men of His time, Lord Chaitanya indeed accepted the austere *sannyasa* order of life in the winter of 1510.

After His *sannyasa*, He wanted to visit Vrindavan, the land of Krishna. For three days and nights He wandered in a trance-like state along the roads of Radha-desh, which, I think, is now called Bardhamana. He was convinced by Nityananda Prabhu to go to Shantipur instead. This is a long story. But at least it can be said that this much happened: He was once again reunited with His Navadvip followers, including His mother, who asked Him to make nearby Jagannath Puri His central headquarters. In this way she would regularly hear of His activities.

So by March, 1510, Mahaprabhu arrived in Jagannath Puri and soon met Sarvabhauma Bhattacharya, a great impersonalist philosopher of the period. Mahaprabhu succeeded in converting the Bhattacharya to His intensely theistic conclusion and this was seen as a great conquest for the Vaishnava movement. By April of this same year, Mahaprabhu began His tour of South India.

Soon after He began His journey, He met Shri Ramananda Roy in Madras on the banks of the Godavari River. This was an important meeting, for here, to His intimate associate, Mahaprabhu revealed His identity as a dual manifestation of Radha and Krishna. More importantly, however, is the dialogue that ensued between Shri Ramananda and Lord Chaitanya, for these conversations embody the most complex theological truths known to man. They are so deep. I recommend that you look at Shrila Prabhupada's translation and commentary of the *Madhya-lila*—it's in his elaborate seventeen-volume masterpiece, *Chaitanya-charitamrita*. A summary can also be found in his *Teachings of Lord Chaitanya*. But let us go on with Lord Chaitanya's story.

That summer—roughly from August to November of 1510—He spent His time at the famous temple of Ranga Swami, at Rangakshetra. There He met the three pious brothers, Vyenkata Bhatta, Tirumalla Bhatta, and the famous Prabodhananda Saraswati. And He also spent time with Vyenkata's little boy, Gopal Bhatta. This boy grew up to be one of Mahaprabhu's most important theologians: Gopal Bhatta Goswami, one of the famous Six Goswamis of Vrindavan.

Then, after continuing His travels throughout South India—which took a total of about two years—He returned to Jagannath Puri. It was the summer of 1511 and He was about twenty-six years of age at this time. This was Ratha-yatra time. Great festival. And by now Mahaprabhu was well-known—a celebrity—all over India. So guests were coming from all over. In this way He spent some time training disciples and showing mercy to admirers. Of course, you'll excuse me for leaving out details, but you wanted only an overview, with dates, and, besides, I'm anxious to get to our present subject of study, the *Shikshashtakam* prayers.

So, to continue, by the fall of 1514, when Mahaprabhu was, oh, about twenty-eight, He decided once again to go to Shri Krishna's land of Vrindavan. On the way He hoped to meet Dabir Khas and Sakara Malik, two important and very learned officials in the Islamic occupational government. They were writing Him letters expressing their dissatisfaction with politics and materialistic life in general. They wanted to surrender to the Bhakti movement. Of course, they were already great devotees, but they wanted to directly work with their Lord and Master. So Mahaprabhu stopped in their town, Ramakeli, on His way to Vrindavan. He met them and accepted them as His dear disciples. They, of course, came to be known as Rupa and Sanatan Goswamis, the chief followers of Shri Chaitanya.

By that summer He was back in Puri, having decided for various reasons that He should hold off His trip to Vrindavan. However, after a few months, He decided that He couldn't take it any longer. So by June 1515, when Mahaprabhu was twenty-nine years old, He went to Vrindavan. Actually, as a side note, my spiritual master, Shrila Prabhupada, also went to Vrindavan for the first time when he was twenty-nine years old, in 1925. So both he and Mahaprabhu entered Vrindavan for the first time, at least according to our external vision, when they were the same age: twenty-nine years old.

Anyway, after visiting all of the holy forests where Krishna engaged in His divine pastimes some 4,500 years earlier, and after bathing in the holy rivers and identifying certain holy places and associating with the various devotees of Braj, Mahaprabhu decided to return to Puri. So by January of 1516, He left Vrindavan via Allahabad, which was then called Prayag. There He spent many months with Rupa Goswami, instructing him in the esoterica of *Rasa-tattva*. He then sent Rupa to Vrindavan and left for Benares on the road to Puri. At Benares He instructed Sanatan Goswami in the philosophy of Krishna consciousness, ultimately telling him also to go to Vrindavan. While in Benares, too, Mahaprabhu converted one of India's most famous if also stubborn mayavadis, Prakashananda Saraswati. When this particular mayavadi came to see Mahaprabhu's perspective, he and his tens of thousands of disciples surrendered to Mahaprabhu's lotus feet.

Having just turned thirty, in the year 1516, Mahaprabhu settled in Puri, never to leave again. So this means that He was to spend the final eighteen years of His manifest pastimes in Puri, after which He left this world, at age forty-eight. It should be noted that by this time He was accepted as a divinity by the mass of people and even by King Prataparudra, who had great influence not only in Orissa but in much of the subcontinent. Great learned Pandits and scholars came to visit and even surrendered to the sankirtan mission. Vallabhacharya came. Guru Nanak came. And as the years passed, Mahaprabhu became more and more thoroughly gripped by *Radha-bhava*, the ecstasy associated with Radharani's essence. *Mahabhava*. In the last few years of His manifest pastimes, Mahaprabhu even exhibited the complete contraction of His bodily limbs, which only manifests in the twelfth state of *Mahabhava*. This is called *Dvadashadasha*, and it is rarely achieved. At this juncture in history, Puri was a center for love of God.

Then, in 1534, He mysteriously vanished into the Tota Gopinath Deity. Or some say the Jagannath Deity. His mood of love in separation became so intense that He could no longer tolerate it. Having completed His manifest pastimes, He disappeared from human vision in order to engage in His eternal *lila* in the celestial Navadvip-dham, the innermost portion of Goloka, in the spiritual sky. After He left, there was political unrest in Puri, which gradually lost importance, at least as the major center of Gaudiya Vaishnavism. Due to the academic proficiency of the Six Goswamis and the missionary zeal of Narottam, Shrinivas, and

Shyamananda, Vrindavan became the new central headquarters, and Gaudiya Vaishnavism thrives there to this day. But that's a completely different story...

Satyaraja Dasa: Anyway, it's running very late. So we'll meet tomorrow and begin with our first discussion of Mahaprabhu's eight verses.

FIRST DISCUSSION: August 9, 1990

Okay. So I think we should discuss the first four verses today and then next week we can continue with the other four verses. In this way we can discuss all eight verses of Shri Chaitanya Mahaprabhu.

From the very first verse, you'll see that Mahaprabhu immediately hones in on the importance of chanting the holy names. This is the essence. But before we explore the all-inclusive significance of spiritual sounds, we should understand the full potency of even material sounds, or vibrations that permeate the material sphere.

Sounds. Their importance should not be underestimated. When sounds are properly used they can change a person's perspective. Totally. All kinds of people rallied together and sang "La Marseillaise" in the French Revolution. "The Horst Wessel Song" fueled the dictatorship of Nazi Germany. "Buddy, Can You Spare a Dime" was the fire-side song of the Great Depression. And "We Shall Overcome" unified the Civil Rights movement. For every era, there is a song, a group of sounds that influenced the day. For the Sixties we may think of the Beatles or Bob Dylan, or, for another segment, perhaps, Jimi Hendrix, and, for still another, the Grateful Dead or the Jefferson Airplane. Sound vibration is integral to our way of perceiving things, and they affect us in ways we know and even in ways we do not know.

We are all aware of the subliminal effect of sound. We commonly use sound for our own dastardly ends. Or sometimes we utilize sounds in a good way, for righteous purposes. But since we lean toward personal sense gratification, we tend to exploit sound. We even tend to cause wars with sound. By the media. By capturing television, radio and newspapers—and by presenting slanted propaganda. We influence war. Those who know exactly how to do it—how to *harness* sound, if you will—they can get what they want out of life. If they're expert, they can easily...motivate people—even *control* people—with the simplest sounds. Words incite riots. Advertisers incite consumers to buy all kinds of things that they don't really need. Words are *that* powerful. Indirect vocabulary. Euphemisms. And then there are the buzz-words, or catch-phrases, sounds that are meant to evoke a particular response. It's quite a developed science.

If the sounds that we are accustomed to are that powerful, what then can be said of the sounds that are beyond our limited sphere of knowledge? If the expert manipulators of conventional sound are able to exploit the world to such a profound degree—or, in some cases, to help the world—perhaps there are sounds beyond our current limited reckoning that can take us further, sounds that can open up new vistas of possiblity.

In fact, proponents of modern science inform us that there *are* sounds that are beyond our reckoning, sounds to which we presently have no access. For example, as human beings we are physically unable to perceive certain portions of the known vibratory spectrum. Although we are extremely sensitive to sound waves of about 1,000 to 4,000 cycles per second (cps), we're all but deaf to sound waves above 20,000 cps. Dogs and cats, on the other hand, can hear up to 60,000 cps, while mice, rats, whales, and dolphins can actually emit and receive sounds well over 100,000 cps. Thus, as human beings, our senses are imperfect and limited. Indeed, even of the sounds we *can* hear—are we really hearing them properly? How much escapes us? Modern science, then, if nothing else, can lead us to at least one inescapable conclusion in regard to sound: we must admit our limitations in this one particular area.

This all leads us to the central teaching of Chaitanya Mahaprabhu, which centers on sound and its most profound dimensions. Basing His teaching on the ancient Vedic texts of India, He tells us, as do the proponents of modern science, that there are sounds that lay far beyond the purview of ordinary sense perception.

Among these uncommon sounds, there are spiritual sounds, according to Lord Chaitanya, and they are called *shabda-brahma.* These sounds have the special potency to fully awaken people from the slumber of materialistic life. The Vedic literature holds that the common, unenlightened person is in a sleep-like state. The analogy is actually quite fitting because until one "wakes up" to reality—abiding reality— one may, at least in a practical sense, appropriately be deemed "asleep."

To further extend the analogy, the most common way to awaken someone is to make some sound. Think about it. The other senses are inefficient in this regard. If a friend is sleeping and you want to wake him up—what's the first thing to do? You may dress yourself quite lavishly and with abundant decoration—but the sleeping person will not take notice. You may even dress in "loud" colors—but it will not be loud enough to awaken our sleeping friend. No. It's clear: the most natural thing is to call out his name until he wakes up.

So this is Mahaprabhu's method, and it is based on the ancient Vedic texts. Actually, the Vedic literature recommends various methods of God realization for different ages. In the Satya-yuga, millions of years ago, the method was meditation. The type of yoga and meditational techniques employed by many today were actually meant for Satya-yuga, when practitioners supposedly lived for many thousands of years. According to the original texts on yoga, it actually takes at least a thousand years to perfect this process. So it is not recommended for Kali-yuga, the current age, when we only live one hundred years—tops.

Then, in Treta-yuga, when natural commodities—gold, silver, all kinds of natural products of the earth—existed in abundance, before the environment was raped, thousands of years before the Industrial Revolution, the method of God realization was sacrifice. Great offerings were made to the Deity. This carried over into Dvapara-yuga as well, when temple worship was the recommended means of God realization.

But in this age, Kali-yuga, chanting is recommended. Mahaprabhu taught:

> *harer nama harer nama*
> *harer nama eva kevalam*
> *kalau nasti-eva nasti-eva*
> *nasti-eva gatir anyata*

"In this age of Kali, there is no other way, no other way, no other way for spiritual progress, other than chanting the holy name, chanting the holy name, chanting the holy name of the Lord." This is further confirmed in *Shrimad Bhagavatam*, in the twelfth canto, where it is mentioned that whatever was achieved by meditation in Satya-yuga, sacrifice in Treta-yuga, and temple worship in Dvapara-yuga—the same thing can be achieved in this age simply by chanting the holy name of the Lord. So this is called the *tarak brahma nam*, or "the name that helps one to cross beyond the ocean of illusion." The various levels of this name, and what one can expect to achieve by chanting it, were revealed in the verses of Lord Chaitanya.

So first I'll give these verses to you in the original Sanskrit, one

by one, and then I'll use Shrila Prabhupada's English translation. I'll try
to explain them in a more or less traditional Gaudiya Vaishnava way so
that you can get a feel for the poetry and at the same time see the depth
of knowledge that is there in these *shlokas*. Okay. So the first one is...

1.

**cheto-darpana-marjanam
bhava-mahadavagni-nirvapanam
shreyah kairava-chandrikavitaranam
vidya-vadhu-jivanam
anandambudhi-vardhanam pratipadam
purnamritasvadanam
sarvatma-snapanam param
vijayate shri-krishna-sankirtanam**

"All glories to the Shri Krishna sankirtan, which cleanses the heart of all
the dust accumulated for years and extinguishes the fire of conditional life,
of repeated birth and death. This sankirtan movement is the prime
benediction for humanity at large because it spreads the rays of the
benediction moon. It is the life of all transcendental knowledge. It increases the ocean of transcendental bliss, and it enables us to fully taste
the nectar for which we are always anxious."

Explanatory Discussion

    Cheto-darpana means "the mirror of the mind." If you let a mirror
sit for many years a great amount of dust accumulates. This is actually our
unfortunate position, isn't it? For countless births we have enhanced our
conditioned state, developing likes and dislikes for millennia. According to
the Vedic tradition there are 8,400,000 species of life, and we desperately
travel through each of them trying to reclaim our original, natural state of
spiritual happiness. So we go through the different bodies, each equipped
with a particular sensual forte.
    None of these bodies are particularly satisfying, though, and
nature is set up in such a way that this subtle point eventually becomes
glaringly obvious to us, especially when we are evolved human beings,

human beings with a spiritual perspective. Then, and only then, do we genuinely see the futility of trying to artificially squeeze pleasure out of material life.

Why artificially? Because material life is not natural for us—we are originally spiritual beings. There is an inherent difference between me and this table. That difference is the soul, the spiritual element. Consciousness. So if I, a spiritual being, try to enjoy matter, I'm like a fish out of water, and, eventually, that becomes very clear. It is at this point, then, that I begin to pursue spiritual pleasure, which is of a higher quality and, more importantly, it lasts. It has substance.

But to reach this point of awareness one requires *marjanam*, or "cleansing." So Mahaprabhu says *"cheto darpana-marjanam."* We must clean the mind of materialistic conditioning. Then what happens? When you cleanse a mirror it can reflect whatever is actually there. So then you can see yourself—who you really are. And you can see God—your relationship with God. These things are clearly seen for one who learns how to clean the mirror of the soul.

This cleansing is done through the holy name of Krishna. Therefore Mahaprabhu says, *vijayate shri krishna-sankirtanam*, or "all glories to the chanting of the holy name of Krishna." Why? Because this chanting is the only real cleansing process. When one learns how to properly chant, under the direction of a bona-fide spiritual master....Oh, there are so many ways to perfect one's chanting. The genuine spiritual teacher will help his disciple avoid the ten offenses. Actually it is a great science. But if one chants properly, then there are seven effects of the holy name. Yes. That is given in this verse by Lord Chaitanya.

The first of the seven effects has already been mentioned: It cleanses the mirror of the mind. Next, it stops the miseries of material existence. Mahaprabhu compares the material world to *mahadavagni*, a "great forest fire." So this fire is completely "extinguished," *nirvapanam*, by the chanting process. That is the second effect of chanting.

Then Mahaprabhu gets particularly poetic. He mentions the *kairava*, which is a special white lotus—sometimes described as a "transcendental lily"—that blooms only at night. You see, the lotus is the emblem of auspiciousness, and Mahaprabhu is herein indicating that just as the moonshine brings forth the tender *kairava*, so also does the holy name spread the moonshine of good fortune and auspiciousness. So this is the third effect that one can expect by the proper chanting of Shri Krishna's name.

Next, the fourth effect—that is *vidya*, or "knowledge." Actually, Mahaprabhu says *vidya-vadhu-jivanam*, which refers to Saraswati, the Goddess of Learning. So it is said that all knowledge comes to one who sincerely chants the holy name of the Lord. It is the life and soul of all education. Actually, what is knowledge really worth if it does not lead to love of God? So, according to Mahaprabhu, a truly sincere chanter has all knowledge, for he has realized the ultimate purport of learning, which is submission to the will of God.

We'll go on. *Anandam-budhi-vardhanam*. The next few words of this *shloka* tell us that sincere chanting can give the highest bliss. Whatever state of happiness you've attained, proper chanting can take you further. The word *vardhanam* means "increasing." So it increases whatever bliss you may have. This is the fifth effect. Actually, this is very important because everyone wants to be happy. It's natural. But Mahaprabhu's claim is that one can actually achieve a superior happiness—superior in terms of quality and quantity—if one learns how to become absorbed in the holy name. It is everlasting and it is joyfully performed. So Mahaprabhu is beckoning us, challenging us. We should call His bluff and try it. We can only come out on top. We don't have to give up our material life. All we have to do is add this chanting to our lives. Then we can see if it actually offers the highest happiness.

The sixth outcome of chanting is that it gives a soothing effect—a cooling feeling. In other words, it gives relief from material life. And this leads to the seventh effect: *Prati-padam purnamritasvada-nam*. It gives the full nectar at every step. Then: *sarvatma-snapanam param*. Yes. At that time, one's whole existence becomes thoroughly bathed in transcendence. So this is it. The sevenfold effect of chanting. No gaps. One feels a constant surge of spiritual pleasure. But one must become adept. This is all in the first verse of Mahaprabhu's *Shikshashtakam* prayers.

2.

namnamakari bahudha
nija-sarva-shaktis
tatrarpita niyamitak
smarane na kalaha
etadrishi tava kripa
bhagavan mamapi
durdaivam idrisham
ihajani nanuragaha

"O my Lord, Your holy name alone can render all benediction to living beings, and thus You have hundreds and millions of names like Krishna and Govinda. In these transcendental names You have invested all Your transcendental energies, and there are no hard and fast rules for chanting these names. O my Lord, out of kindness You enable us to easily approach You by chanting Your holy names, but I am so unfortunate that I have no attraction for them."

Explanatory Discussion

So this is the second of Mahaprabhu's eight verses. It begins with an affirmation of the fact that everything can be gotten from the holy name Itself, or *Himself*, since the holy name is herein revealed to be nondifferent from the Lord's own self-existent nature. Lord Chaitanya expresses this by saying *nija-sarva-shakti*—all of the Lord's potencies are existing in His holy Name. In other words, the Lord and His name are nondifferent. This is the nature of Absolute phenomena. We, on the other hand, are accustomed to relative phenomena, and so we cannot conceive of an object and its name being nondifferent. In the relative world, the name is just a symbol—an abstract representation. If I think of water, for example, the thought alone cannot quench my thirst. The substance water and the word water are two completely different phenomena. I could chant "water, water, water" until I'm blue in the face—but my thirst will not go away. That is the nature of the relative world. But the Absolute realm is just the opposite. There, a name and the thing it represents are identical. If I chant "Krishna, Krishna, Krishna," I'm actually in contact with Him.

This principle was explained in complex theological terminology by the Six Goswamis of Vrindavan. To state it simply, they called it *nama-naminor-adwaita*, which means, literally, "the nondifference between the Named one and the Name." Jiva Goswami went so far as to say, *bhagavat swarupam eva nam*, or "the Name is the actual essence of the Lord." In fact, Mahaprabhu taught that the holy name is a type of *avatar*, that is to say, it is "the Lord in the form of syllables": *varna-rupenavataro 'yam*.

If you study the Judaeo-Christian tradition, too, you will find that, in ancient times, this was also understood. For example, there is great instruction in "Our Father who art in Heaven—hallowed be Thy Name." Not only is this encouragement for chanting God's name, but, also, the word "hallowed" didn't always mean what it means today. Today it means "sacred." We say that the name of God is sacred. But originally the word *hallowed* meant *whole*. The name of God was considered complete. So "Hallowed be Thy name" meant that God's name was complete in Itself. Yes, full of His own potency, as Mahaprabhu says.

This is true of all genuinely spiritual sound vibrations. It is in fact a nonsectarian principle. Therefore, Mahaprabhu says *namnam akari bahudha*—that there are various kinds of names for the Lord. It is not restricted to Sanskrit or Bengali. No. Any name that actually describes God is totally spiritual and is thus nondifferent from His very essence. The names of Krishna and Govinda are particularly special names, referring to God's highest and original feature in the divine kingdom, in the spiritual world, and for this reason, Prabhupada, the translator, has used these two names as prime examples, even though the names do not specificaly appear in this verse. Actually, by using the word *bahudha*, Mahaprabhu is indicating that all genuine names of God are acceptable: Allah, Adonai, El, HaShem, Buddha, Christ—therefore it is said that God has hundreds and millions of names.

All of the world's major religious traditions elucidate this same principle and encourage adherents to chant these names, even if, in practice, it is hardly followed. In fact, all religions emphasize the chanting process as the prime means for developing God consciousness. For example, King David, of the Bible, preached: "From the rising of the sun until its setting, the Lord's name is to be praised." (*Psalms*, 113:3) Saint Paul said that "everyone who calls upon the name of the Lord shall be saved." (*Romans*, 10:13) In this way, the potency of the name is endorsed even in the Western religious traditions.

Not only can it be said that there are multifarious names through which one can approach the Lord, but there are no hard and fast rules for chanting these names. No *niyamitah*, or "restrictions," and no special time, *kalah*, as Mahaprabhu says. Anytime. Anywhere. You see, certain Vedic *mantras* and certain prayers within other religious traditions as well—they have definite ways of chanting, according to time, place, and circumstance. But the name of God is special and is to be chanted *constantly*, as Mahaprabhu again confirms in the next verse: *kirtaniya sada hari*. Actually, this command is also in the Bible: "Pray ceaselessly." This is in the first part of *Thessalonians* (5.17). Not vain repetition—the Bible warns us about that. But pure, sincere chanting, or prayerful chanting. Calling out to God with love and devotion. There are no rules and regulations to restrict that. That is beyond legislation. It is from the heart. Therefore, taking the position of the perfect devotee, teaching us how to pray in the proper mood, Mahaprabhu thanks the Lord for showing us this mercy in relation to the holy name.

But just because the Lord is merciful enough to give us an unlimited variety of names, and to excuse us for offenses, informing us that there are no hard and fast rules for this chanting, we should not by that become exploitative. We should not abuse His kindness by chanting in an insincere way. No. We should be respectful, grateful, and humble—always anxious to become more and more sincere or adept in our chanting. We should always remember that despite the Lord's kindness, we are still so fallen that we continue to have no taste for the name. Lord Chaitanya, taking our position, teaches us exactly what our perceptions should be about our own relationship with the holy name. He says, *durdaivam idrisham ihajani nanuragaha:* "It is my great misfortune that I was born without any attraction or attachment for the holy name." Any questions?

Question: If chanting is an inherent feature of the soul—if it is natural to call out to God in love and devotion—why do we have no attraction? Why, as Lord Chaitanya says, do we not have any natural attachment to this chanting?

Satyaraja Dasa: This is a very good question. Actually, you'll remember that Mahaprabhu answered this in His very first verse: We've accumulated dust—conditioning—on the mirror of the consciousness. For this reason we have no taste, or, rather, we've developed perverted tastes, so to speak. We've developed attraction and attachment for things of this world, and we've lost, or, let us say that we've covered over, our natural attraction and attachment for things of the spirit, at least to the degree that we are conditioned.

You see, externally it may appear as though our taste for chanting develops gradually—that it is an acquired taste. But actually it is our *original* taste, the taste of the soul. It is our current personality that is actually *acquired*—it is unnatural. In this connection, the etymology of the word "personality" is very interesting. It's traced back to the root *personna*, which originally referred to the mask that an actor wore during a dramatic performance. It wasn't his real identity. It was a part he played. Similarly we've developed gross materialistic personalities, colored by the three modes of material nature, goodness, passion, and ignorance. And when we finally purify ourselves through certain reliable prescribed austerities, chief amongst which is the chanting of the holy name, we begin to remember our original personality. We begin to remember who we were before we adopted our external personna. This is called self-realization.

Bhaktivinode Thakur, a great saint in the Chaitanyite line, has also commented, specifically in regard to this verse by Lord Chaitanya—actually, he directly answers your question. He says that there are basically four obstacles to our attraction and attachment to the holy name. First, he points to *swarupa-bram*, or one's "mistaken identity." As soon as we are born into this world, we identify with the body and mind, totally oblivious to our real identity as the soul within. Still, an honest person will admit that "I don't know where I came from. I don't know where I'm going. Since this is true, I've got a deep suspicion that I don't even really know who I am now." [laughter] If a person can admit this much—that is a good beginning for spiritual life.

Next, Bhaktivinode mentions *asad-trishna*, or "evil propensities." Due to conditioning we become selfish. Where there is self, there is self interest. That is natural. But the more covered we get, the more our sense of self interest becomes exaggerated, and we develop an exploitative mentality, especially if we are conditioned by a preponderance of passion and ignorance. These are the evil propensities that tend to make our heart very hard, and we then have no patience for chanting the holy name. We develop an aversion for supplicating some distant "Supreme Being," and we lose whatever spiritual taste we may have had. Or it becomes covered, as I have mentioned earlier. Actually, *hriddoybolla*, or "weakness of heart," which is the third obstacle mentioned by Bhaktivinode, is closely related to this principle of evil propensities. It takes strength to overcome one's conditioning, which is very deep-rooted. And one must purify one's consciousness before one can even really understand why it is ultimately in one's own self interest to become free from the misconceptions associated with mundane existence.

The fourth and final obstacle mentioned by Shrila Bhaktivinode Thakur in this connection is *aparadh*, or "offenses." I've made a list here of the ten major offenses and these can be circulated so you can get some idea. Anyway, this is the thing. Therefore, you can see that it is a great science and, in answer to your question, the Gaudiya Vaishnavas do have an elaborate theology about why the conditioned living entity may feel as though he has no taste for the holy name. Hmmm. So these are Bhaktivinode Thakur's statements on Mahaprabhu's second verse of the *Shikshashtakam* prayers.

3.

trinad api sunichena
taror iva sahishnuna
amanina manadena
kirtaniyah sada hari

"One should chant the holy name of the Lord in a humble state of mind, thinking oneself lower than the straw in the street; one should be more tolerant than a tree, devoid of all sense of false prestige and should be ready to offer all respect to others. In such a state of mind one can chant the holy name of the Lord constantly."

Explanatory Discussion

Here, in Mahaprabhu's third verse, He continues on the theme of humility. He had ended the last verse by bemoaning the fact that He had no taste for the holy name. This is the humility that a devotee will naturally develop. In fact, this is carried over into this current verse, the third verse, which now goes so far as to say that one must chant in a state of *amanina*. That is to say: one must chant without being even slightly puffed up by pride and arrogance. This is no easy accomplishment. But this is what it takes to actually enter into the mysteries of the holy name.

We must consider ourselves *trinad-api-sunichena*, or, literally, "more down-trodden than the lowly grass." And we must have *taroh sahishnuna*—the full tolerance of a tree! If you hit a tree or treat it disrespectfully—it will still give you all the shade you want. It tolerates scorching heat and stands in the rain. Most of all, despite any inconvenience, it still gives shelter to others. This is the main thing that one can learn from a tree.

Of course, it may be said that a tree actually has no choice, and we do. But the tenor of this verse is that one must put oneself in that *mood* of selflessness. "I'm not so special." In this way. Only if we feel ourselves to be in this rather lowly condition will we be ready to offer *manadena*, or "respects to all living beings." This is the mood of a devotee. Now, someone may say that this is too self-effacing. A devotee may lose self-esteem, integrity. And how can one be a productive person—or even serve the Lord, for that matter!—if one is feeling oneself to be in a terrible lowly position?

One should understand that Mahaprabhu's method must be practiced with practicality. If one has a severe ego problem, wherein one feels totally useless, so much so that one cannot do any tangible service or cannot even chant, for that matter—such a person would do well to take pride in the fact that they are an aspiring devotee of Krishna, and that's really a great position—because Krishna, God, is the greatest. By recognizing that one has found the path of God consciousness in this life—among so many who haven't found this path—one should be genuinely happy and grateful. They certainly shouldn't be so self-indulgent that they spend all their time worrying about how useless they are. Meditation on the fact that one has found the path of spiritual life and the association of devotees can help one who is suffering from an acute inferiority complex.

Truth be told, though, people don't generally suffer from this problem. People tend to lean in the other direction. We generally think that we are God's gift to creation. *These* types of ego problems are much more prominent. In fact, religious or "spiritual" people, too—in some cases *especially* religious people—they are guilty of a sort of "holier than thou" attitude. So, to compensate, we are asked to go in the other direction. "You are puffed-up—you think you're so great. So now try and realize how small you actually are!"

And, in point of fact, we *are* very tiny. Out of all the countless universes, we are in one small universe. Out of all the planets and stars in this universe, we are on one particular planet. Given the limited dimensions of this planet, there are many countries. And of all those countries, I am in one. This country is made up of many states and those states of many cities. Of all these cities, I am in one particular city. In this city, there are many neighborhoods, and of them all, I am in one particular neighborhood. In my neighborhood, there are many streets—I am on only one street. Then, on this street, there are many houses and apartment buildings. I happen to be in one particular apartment building. In this building there are many apartments of all shapes and sizes. I am in one of them. And even in my one apartment, there are numerous living beings—such as insects, microbes, et cetera. I am one living being among all of these living beings. And I am thinking: "Oh, I'm *so* important."

So if we are a little introspective, a little contemplative, we will see our minuscule place in this universe. It is humbling. If we think about God's greatness, especially, we will realize how small we actually are. And there are definite advantages to realizing our tiny position. We don't become the loser. Think about it. To be more tolerant than a tree....hmmm. This would actually be quite useful. How often we lose our temper or get angry about petty little things. If we could develop tolerance we can rise beyond these problems. If you think about it, most of our problems come from having an inflated conception of who we are. Just imagine. If we were genuinely humble, then we would not get angry every time something didn't go our way. And we would be sincerely grateful every time it did.

Then, if we can attain this level, we would have a peaceful mind. In this way we could chant the holy name without any disturbance. Or, as Mahaprabhu says, *kirtaniya sada hari*—we could chant constantly. Why? Because our mind would be free. *Mantra* means "mind freedom," or "mind release." So to properly chant a *mantra* one must have a free mind. Actually, it has two sides: one must have a basically free mind to at least begin chanting—otherwise one won't even want to start—and then by chanting one's mind can go further, attaining new heights of freedom— spiritual freedom. So this is alluded to in this verse.

4.

na dhanam na janam na sundarim
kavitam va jagadish kamaye
mama janmani jamanishvare
bhavatad bhaktir ahoituki tvayi

"O almighty Lord, I have no desire to accumulate wealth, nor do I desire to enjoy beautiful women, nor do I want any number of followers. I only want Your causeless devotional service in my life birth after birth."

Explanatory Discussion

This verse establishes the exclusivity of purpose that is

necessary for proper chanting of the holy name. Single-minded determination. The *Gita* also says that one must be *vyavasaya-atmika*, or "resolute on the path of God consciousness." Hmmm....What is that verse? Oh:

bhogaishvarya-prasaktanam
tayapahrita-chetasam
vyavasayatmika buddhih
samadhau na vidhiyate

"In the minds of those who are too attached to sense enjoyment and material opulence, and who are bewildered by such things, the resolute determination for devotional service to the Supreme Godhead does not take place." (B.G. 2:44)

So this is like a sister verse to Mahaprabhu's fourth *shloka*—it contains all of the same elements. Mahaprabhu says that He doesn't want money; He doesn't want followers; He doesn't want beautiful women. No. He doesn't want any material enjoyment at all. Why? Because if He did want such enjoyment then the resolute determination for practicing devotional service would not take place. And He *only* wants pure devotional service. He is showing the resolute determination that is required. If we are divided, if we have some separate interest—we are finished. We will not get the desired goal. We want *prema bhakti*—love of God. We want *ahoituki bhakti*—totally unmotivated and uninterrupted devotional service.

In His conversations with Ramananda Roy, Mahaprabhu rejects *swadharma-charan*, or external religious observances; He rejects *krishna-karmarpan*, or acts that are even directed toward Krishna; He rejects *karma-mishra bhakti*, or the type of devotion that is mixed with fruitive intentions; He even rejected *gyana-mishra-bhakti*, or devotion polluted by a preponderance of knowledge. These things are laudable, no doubt, but Lord Chaitanya was only able to endorse pure, unmotivated spiritual love, beyond even *gyan-shunya-bhakti*—or devotion that does not have even a hint of anything else. It is completely unalloyed—not polluted by even the most subtle tinge of needless knowledge. It is pure.

So this is what He is endorsing in this verse. *Mama janmani jamanishvare*: "Birth after birth, let me just serve Your lotus feet." In what way? How would I like to serve You? *Bhavatad bhaktir ahoituki tvayi*: "Let me serve You without any ulterior motivation. Let me serve You in a completely pure way." This is the thing.

Question: But it can't be artificial. What if I want to pursue spiritual life but I am not ready to be totally devoted? What if I *do* have separate interests but I nonetheless want to try the chanting process?

Satyaraja Dasa: So? There is no harm. Mahaprabhu has already said that there are no hard and fast rules. In fact, unless one begins—and in the beginning it is likely that one will chant offensively—how can one possibly graduate to higher levels of spiritual attainment? So we must begin. Whatever level we are on—it is all right. But Mahaprabhu is showing us a higher level. And, in fact, if we are maturing properly, we will see that we are gradually losing our taste for sense enjoyment and we are developing a taste for spiritual pleasure, a taste for the divine name, for sacred vegetarian food, for spiritual painting, for Deity worship, for *kirtan*—divinely inspired song and dance.

This is what Mahaprabhu is showing in this verse: If you are actually developing a taste for the holy name, you will naturally develop a distaste for material enjoyment. Your material fever goes down. In this way you can ascertain your progress. Just like when you are sick. If your fever goes down, oh, then you know you are getting well. Krishna says:

vishaya vinivartante
niraharasya dehinah
rasa-varjam raso 'pyasya
param drishtva nivartate

"Although an embodied soul may restrict himself from sense enjoyment, the taste for it remains. He can genuinely give up the lower taste only when he has experienced the higher taste." (B.G. 2:59)

So, this is the point. When one understands the need for spiritual life and the need to curtail material excesses, one begins to practice certain penance and austerity. People may become vegetarian; or they may fast on certain days; they may chant a prescribed number of holy names on the rosary; whatever. But they are doing it by using their higher intelligence. Not because it necessarily "feels good." It is like a calculated austerity. One foregoes some short-range pleasure in favor of a considerably more promising and substantial long-range pleasure. This is the beginning of spiritual life.

But then something interesting happens. *Param drishtva nivartate.* One experiences a higher taste. Then, as Mahaprabhu says in this verse, one doesn't care for money, the opposite sex, fame, or recognition. No. Enjoying these things is like chewing the chewed. They have lost their flavor. Rather, one's senses are now alive to spiritual life. They perceive new dimensions. They can now embrace reality in a more substantial way. You are finally awake! Alive! Vibrant! The entire spiritual world opens up, and, now, possibly for the first time, you can actually see the material world in perspective. So this is Krishna consciousness. This is the initial effect of the holy name...

Question: What is the ultimate effect of the holy name?

Satyaraja Dasa: To develop pure love of God. That we will discuss next week.

SECOND DISCUSSION: September 6, 1990

I am sorry it took so long to arrange this second meeting. Some of you are anxious to hear about Shri Chaitanya Mahaprabhu's final four verses, I know, and, by Shri Krishna's grace, we can now continue. So maybe we should just get right into it. For those of you who were not here during our last meeting, I have written a brief synopsis of those previous talks. The fifth verse begins like this:

5.

**ayi nandatanuja kinkaram
patitam mam vishame bhavambudho
kripaya tava pada-pankaja
sthita-dhulisadrisham vichintaya**

"O Son of Maharaj Nanda [Krishna], I am Your eternal servitor, yet somehow or other I have fallen into the ocean of birth and death. Please pick me up from this ocean of death and place me as one of the atoms of Your lotus feet."

Explanatory Discussion

I would like to begin with a word of caution: Mahaprabhu is Krishna Himself—God—but in order to teach the highest path of spiritual mysticism, devotional service, He comes in the form of His own devotee. Therefore, in this verse, especially, He speaks as if He were an ordinary conditioned soul. This is His special mercy. He is commiserating, showing us that He understands, and that we can still attain the Supreme Destination, even in our very fallen condition.

You see, Krishna came at the end of Dvapara-yuga, about 5,000 years ago, and He spoke *Bhagavad-gita* for the enlightenment of all living beings. Many people misunderstood His teachings, however, and so He therefore came again, in Kali-yuga, about 500 years ago, just to show us by His personal example how one can actually live according to the principles of the *Gita*. Mahaprabhu shows the practical application of His own teachings.

But make no mistake: If the teacher shows the student how to practice writing the alphabet by his own example, we should not think that he is doing it to learn himself. Although Mahaprabhu, in this verse, posed as a devotee who is bewildered about his place in this world— He says He is *bhava-ambudho*, or "in the ocean of nescience"—we should be aware that He is herein just showing us how to admit our own fallen condition. He is actually teaching by His own example. This is quite clear, for advanced spiritual masters throughout history and the scriptures themselves vouch for His total divinity. So we should not be bewildered by His apparent splashing in "the ocean of nescience."

Anyway, it is highly significant that this verse begins *ayi nanda-tanuja*, for the Lord always likes to be remembered in relation to His devotees, and so Mahaprabhu is showing how to do this. He is calling Krishna the "Son of Maharaj Nanda." When Shri Krishna descended to this earth 5,000 years ago, He came, as always, with His associates and paraphernalia and abode. So the devotee Nanda always plays the role of Krishna's father. In this way, Krishna relishes a relationship with this particular devotee. In the ultimate analysis, of course, Krishna is eternal, and so the terms "father" and "mother" sort of lose all meaning, at least as we relate to such concepts here in this realm.

But the reason such relationships can exist here at all is because they have their original counterpart in that realm, in the spiritual realm. So this is called *rasa* theology, and it is very developed in our Chaitanyite Vaishnavism. Briefly stated, in one's original, or constitutional, spiritual position, one may interact with God in one of five primary relationships. For example, one can relate as a neutral party, which is called *shanta-rasa*; as a servant, which is called *dasya-rasa;* or as a friend, which is called *sakhya-rasa*; as a parent, which is called *vatsalya rasa*; or as a transcendental lover—and that is known as *madhurya-rasa*. So this is a very important tenet of Mahaprabhu's teaching and it is dealt with at length in the writings of the Goswamis.

In this, the fifth verse of *Shikshashtakam*, Mahaprabhu is addressing Krishna in relationship to His great devotee Nanda Maharaj, who is in *vatsalya-rasa*, parenthood, and this brings great pleasure to the Lord. But what does Mahaprabhu tell Krishna, the Divine Son of Nanda Maharaj? He says that "I am Your fallen servant—eternally." Yes. We are eternally Krishna's servants. We are part and parcel of God. This is the thing. And Mahaprabhu is bringing out a very logical conclusion: "Since I am originally Shri Krishna's servant, I should return to this service. It is my natural, constitutional position."

And I should return to this service in a humble way. Mahaprabhu says *kripaya tava pada-pankaja sthita-dhuli-sadrisham vichintaya*, which means "Please be merciful unto me and allow me to be a particle of dust at Your lotus feet." This is the mood. We should not think: "All right. I will be Your humble servant. But only if I can make an important place for myself amongst Your devotees. Only if I can take a prominent role." No. Mahaprabhu has taught the proper mood: *gopi bhartu pada-kamalayor dasa-dasanudasa*. We do not approach directly. We aspire to be servants of the servants of the servants of the gopis, the revered cowherd maidens. But we are very removed. Indirect servants. The more removed, the better. It is a humble position. "Oh, the servants of Krishna are so great. I am not worthy of their shoes. Not even the dust from their feet." So Mahaprabhu teaches us to approach God with this humility—*dhuli-sadrisham*, like the particle of dust.

Actually, many exalted devotees in the annals of Vaishnava history have also prayed in this way. For example, Lord Brahma (the first created being and the founder of Mahaprabhu's lineage) prayed to take birth as anything—a rock, a leaf—in the forest of Vrindavan. Why? So the great devotees of Krishna, who always reside in Vrindavan, might perchance step on him, so he can get the dust of their feet. Brahma's prayer is recorded in the tenth canto of the *Shrimad Bhagavatam*.

Uddhava, too, wanted such a benediction. He was the greatest of the Yadavas, but still he knew that the love of the gopis was superior. For this reason, he wanted to take the dust from their feet on his head. But he was too humble to ask them. So he also prayed to

THE EIGHT PRAYERS OF LORD CHAITANYA

take birth as a creeper in the land of Vrindavan. In this way he thought that the gopis would perhaps dance on his head, and he would receive the mercy of Krishna.

It should be understood that whether one is an atom of dust at Shri Krishna's feet, as Mahaprabhu prays, or whether one is an atom of dust at the feet of Krishna's pure devotee—there is no difference. It is this mood of humility that is sought after by the devotees, and by attaining this level of humility, they can attain the mercy of Shri Krishna.

Brahma actually received the benediction of being born as Haridas Thakur, one of Mahaprabhu's most intimate followers and the great teacher of the holy name. And Uddhava took birth as Paramananda Puri, one of the peers of Mahaprabhu's spiritual master. So they received the topmost benediction—they gained entrance into the pastimes of Lord Shri Chaitanya Mahaprabhu.

6.

nayanam galadashrudharaya
vadanam gadgadaruddhaya gira
pulakair nichitam vapuhkada
tava namagrahane bhavishyati

"O my Lord, when will my eyes be decorated with tears of love flowing constantly when I chant Your holy name? When will my voice choke up, and when will the hairs of my body stand on end at the recitation of Your name?"

Explanatory Discussion

Mahaprabhu is here referring to *sattvika-bhavas*, or the ecstatic bodily transformations that occur due to one's developing love of God. *Chaitanya-charitamrita* tells us that perspiration, trembling, hairs standing on end, tears, faltering of the voice, fainting, madness, melancholy, patience, pride, joy, and humility—these are natural symptoms of ecstatic love for God, and they cause a devotee to dance and, yes, even to float in the ocean of transcendental bliss. These symptoms sometimes occur while an adept engages in chanting the holy name of the Lord. But such an adept may sometimes conceal such symptoms so as not to confuse the neophyte practitioner. Rupa Goswami, too, in his *Bhakti-rasamrita-sindhu*, has scientifically outlined these *sattvika-bhavas* so a devotee can ascertain his own level of advancement.

In this verse, Mahaprabhu zeros in on three particular *sattvika-bhavas* as representative of all the rest. *Nayanam galad-ashru-dharaya:* streams of tears running down from the eyes. Then, *vadanam gadgada-ruddhaya gira*—the voice falters; one becomes all choked up. And *pulakair nichitam vapuh*—the hairs on the body will stand erect. A devotee should anticipate such symptoms. As Mahaprabhu says in this verse: *kada bhavishyati*—"When will this occur?"

The answer, of course, is that these symptoms occur when one is approaching the dawn of true love. *Bhava*. Otherwise, we only have experience of the mundane counterparts. Crying, faltering of the voice, bodily hairs standing erect—such phenomena have material counterparts, usually associated with some degree of sentimentality and exaggerated emotionalism. But the *sattvika-bhavas* that are described here are quite different. They are completely spiritual, and one who is properly trained in the scriptures under a bona-fide spiritual master can recognize the difference.

Question: Is it really such a big deal? I mean, let's say that someone does mistake these ecstatic symptoms for something material, won't he still make progress in spiritual life? What difference does it make? Besides, crying, hair standing on end, perspiration—these are common physical manifestations with explanations in modern science. My own mother goes through these changes every time one of my sisters gets married! Forgive me for being so facetious, but maybe these *spiritual* bodily transformations are the same signs of emotionalism we see in our day-to-day life, but simply more intensified.

Satyaraja Dasa: Definitely not. After carefully studying the tradition I can say this with great certainty. But if *you* wanted to know, you would need to study it at length. You see, it is a science. And like in any other science, there are certain laws of function. If one is properly trained in the scriptures by a bona-fide representative of the genuine disciplic succession, then one can understand the importance of the *sattvika-*

bhavas and whether or not they are authentic.

You see it is very different from the mundane symptoms as experienced by your mother. [laughter] When we speak of tears flowing from the eyes or hair standing on end—you can only visualize their material counterpart. But to recognize the genuine ecstatic symptoms—that requires training. Of course, even the overt manifestations of spiritual emotions are actually quite different than their material counterpart. Tears, for instance, flow as if they are shooting out from a syringe! You have never seen such a thing, have you? Neither will you see such a thing in the personality of your mother. [laughter] So these are the spiritual symptoms. When the tears are cold it is a symptom of spiritual jubilation. When they are hot, it is a manifestation of spiritual indignation, or anger. The eyes turn an other-worldly reddish color or sometimes a frightening white. So, you see, it is quite different than the material counterpart. And one who is trained to recognize these things can never be deceived in spiritual life.

Besides, it's not just a question of bodily symptoms. The *sattvika-bhavas* are just one aspect. There are the *vibhavas*, too, or the "excitants" of a spiritual relationship with God. And then there are the *anubhavas*, or the "ensuants" of the relationship And there are also *vyabhichari-bhavas*, or "auxiliary emotions." These *bhavas* are unique in each individual according to that individual's very distinct relationship with Krishna. And one who is trained in spiritual life can detect the particulars of a person's eternal relationship with God by learning how to observe these things. So it is a great science. Anyway, this is all quite complicated. It is known as the advanced stage. The *sattvika-bhavas*—that is a long way off. There are more practical signposts to see if one is advancing properly: Are you losing the taste for material life? Are you developing the taste for service to God? Are you developing cleanliness, truthfulness, austerity, mercy? These are the grassroots transformations that one should observe in the beginning. Preliminary advancement. But even this part is a science. And then, when one actually advances—*then* the *sattvika-bhavas* may take place.

The *sattvika-bhavas*, especially, are there so one can know that he is making progress. Otherwise, how would you know if you're actually advancing spiritually or if you are just deluded? You may be brainwashed. This is the answer. By scientifically analyzing the signposts or the things you can expect along the way, the followers of Mahaprabhu have methodically outlined a very objective spiritual science. In this way, for one who undergoes the proper training, it is virtually impossible to be cheated. One who pursues spiritual life properly, according to the outlines of the Goswamis, will know exactly what the *sattvika-bhavas* mean, and just when they are actually authentic spiritual signs or just mundane counterparts.

Actually, once someone tastes this *Prema-bhakti*, even for a moment, then nothing can take its place. This is the point. This is the proof that it is the highest thing. All classes of transcendentalists are anxious to get this *Prema-bhakti*. Gross materialists, of course, have their own peculiar domain of pleasure—crude, unfulfilling pleasure. Pleasure that is actually painful in the long run. This is the rock bottom variety. There is a higher level of material pleasure. Higher than the gross materialists are the *gyanis*, or those who are on a more subtle platform, somewhat more refined. Their pleasure is more sophisticated and it usually lasts longer as well.

Higher still is the pleasure of the impersonalist, called "*brahmananda*"—this is where spiritual happiness begins. But the most coveted goal is *Prema-bhakti*, love for Krishna, and all of the others, whether they know it or not, are actually hankering after the intense pleasure that comes from this genuine state of Krishna consciousness. This pleasure is so very intense that, once having tasted it, one cannot live without it. It is maddening. The feeling of separation is described as *that* overwhelming. But we are getting too far ahead of ourselves. This divine madness of separation, known as *viraha-bhakti*, is revealed in the next verse of the *Shikshashtakam* prayers.

7.

**yugayitam nimeshena
chakshusha pravrishayitam
shunyayitam jagat-sarvam
govinda-virahena me**

"O Govinda! Feeling Your separation, I am considering a moment to be like twelve years or more. Tears are flowing from my eyes like torrents of rain, and I am feeling all vacant in this world due to Your absence."

Explanatory Discussion

Here, in Chaitanya Mahaprabhu's seventh verse, we are allowed to witness the internal struggle of a soul who is nearing the highest levels of perfection. As Mahaprabhu, in the previous verses, has played the part of souls who are aspiring after perfection, here He shows a soul who is actually experiencing the first stages of genuine Krishna consciousness, of love of God. Here He continues on the theme of *viraha-bhakti*, or "devotion in separation." This is much sought after—for love in separation nourishes love in union. You see, when one reaches some genuine modicum of accomplishment on the path of pure love of God, he experiences two levels: *sambhoga*, or "devotion in union," and *vipralambha*, which is also known as *viraha-bhakti*, or "devotion in separation." When this latter level reaches full intensity, there is union. Separation is the key ingredient for intensity, even when there is union.

For example, once, when Radha and Krishna were performing their divine pastimes together, a large black bee flew into their vicinity. Now, it is to be understood that Krishna is sometimes known as Madhusudana because He killed the demon known as Madhu. But a bumble-bee is also known as Madhusudana because *madhu* also means "honey." Anyway, when Krishna saw the bee, He jokingly said, "Radhe, watch out! That bee may sting you!" Radharani became frightened and ran into Krishna's arms. When She did this, Krishna lovingly joked with Her again, making a play on one of His own names. He said, "Radhe, there is no longer any reason to fear. Madhusudana is already gone." Of course, Krishna was referring to the fact that the bee had already left, but when Radhika even considered the other meaning—that Krishna was gone—She was totally gripped by *vipralambha-bhava*, or the loving mood of separation, even though She was right there in Krishna's arms. So this is the intensity of love in separation. And She appreciated Krishna even more when She began to consider His absence. So this is one sense of it.

So Mahaprabhu begins this seventh *shloka* by addressing Krishna as "Govinda" or as one who pleases the senses. In other words, one's senses become assaulted by separation, even in this world. Every part of the body aches. One cannot eat, sleep—it's called the blues, isn't it? Everyone knows it! It drives us crazy! Separation leads to madness. I would say that most forms of madness come from separation. The materialist goes mad because he is separated from the objects of his sense gratification, isn't it? His wife leaves him or dies; or his business folds; or he loses his money; or his home. He's *separated* from these things, and it hurts. That's material separation, and it's intense. It drives people mad. Now, spiritual separation leads to divine madness, or *divya-maad*, as well, and Mahaprabhu is a prime example of this. But a unique thing about spiritual separation is that it is not a nasty experience. Because it is spiritual it is Absolute, and that means that separation and union are but opposite sides of the same coin. They are but variations in the spiritual pursuit of Krishna's pleasure. Still, the *vipralambha* variation is a type of spiritual longing that drives the devotee mad with love, and so Mahaprabhu asks for relief—it is *that* intense. "Oh Govinda—please relieve my senses!" .

Question: But since it is part of the divine play, why does the devotee hanker so much? He knows that the Lord is merciful and will eventually reunite with him. The Lord is just enticing him with this separation...

Satyaraja Dasa: Yes. I was about to explain that. You see, knowledge does not suffice. Spiritual relationship, *rasa*, supersedes knowledge. Just like that story of Radharani and the bumblebee. She *knew* that Krishna was right there in Her arms. She had this knowledge—direct experiential knowledge! But, still, Her emotions became swept away in this *vipralambha-rasa*, in separation. Why? Because it is the sweetest thing. It is actually the most cherished goal. Only if you really appreciate Krishna can you appreciate the mood of separation and all it offers.

So, you are asking why separation should be taken so seriously despite the knowledge that one can be reunited with the Lord in due course. So I've given one answer—I've explained that knowledge, in and of itself, is not enough. Another perspective on this same issue is revealed by Mahaprabhu in this very verse. When one hankers to be reunited with the Lord, which is called *sambhoga-rasa*, then each moment appears *yugayitam*, or like a great millennium. It seems endless. Yes. Elsewhere, Mahaprabhu says it seems that *divasa na yaya*, that "a day never ends." A *yuga* is sometimes defined as consisting of a minimum of twelve years, so Shrila Prabhupada, the translator, has rendered it as "each moment appears to be like twelve years or more." But usually a *yuga* is considered to be many thousands of years. It is a lengthy timespan that is difficult to accommodate. So Mahaprabhu prays to be relieved of this, to be relieved of this lengthy wait. "I want to be reunited with Krishna—now! I can't take it anymore" This is His mood, His goal. And the urgency of this desire makes it necessary for a devotee to take separation very seriously.

Question: Is this the point of spiritual evolution when the ecstatic symptoms occur?

Satyaraja Dasa: Yes. This is also revealed in this same verse. Mahaprabhu says that due to this separation, He experiences *pravrishayitam*—tears flow from His eyes like torrents of rain. This is the symptom of ecstasy. He says that His eyes become *varshara meghapraya*, or they become just like clouds in the rainy season. The tears of these great devotees are like great monsoon rains, and they alleviate the suffering of novices in Krishna consciousness. One traditional analogy comes to mind: In India, when the hot weather appears, it dries up the cooling waters—especially small puddles—and it may scorch the lotuses that live there. The devotees are compared to those lotuses, and they feel a similar scorching effect due to separation from the Lord. But the great devotees, in this same separation, are crying like the monsoon rains, and it is said that they are soothing their brother and sister lotuses by their generous rain.

Sometimes, the devotee in separation feels as if he's being slowly consumed by a terrible fire. But he knows that Krishna would not really do that to him, and so the sincere devotee generally reasons that "Krishna is doing this to me just to test my love." This is especially the mood of Shrimati Radharani, who is the devotee in separation par excellence. But Radharani goes so far as to say, "Perhaps it's better to disregard Him! If Krishna is going to put Me through such tests, then I want nothing to do with Him." Of course, as soon as She feels like this, She is besieged with mixed emotions. The genuine characteristics of Her natural love once again manifest within Her pure heart. The diverse ecstatic symptoms of envy, great eagerness, humility, zeal, and supplication all become manifest at once. In that exalted mood, Radharani's mind becomes transcendentally agitated, and therefore She speaks in a very distinct way to Her gopi friends. It was in this same spirit that Mahaprabhu uttered the next and final verse of *Shikshashtikam*, and when the verse indeed came from His lips, He was totally overtaken by the identity of Radharani.

8.

ashlishya va padaratam pinashtu mam
adarshananmarmahatam karotu va
yatha tatha va vidadhatu lampato
mat-prana-nathas tu sa eva naparaha

"I know no one but Krishna as my Lord, and He shall remain so even if He handles me roughly in His embrace or makes me brokenhearted by not being present before me. He is completely free to do anything and everything, for He is always my worshipful Lord unconditionally."

Explanatory Discussion

Mahaprabhu, in the mood of Radharani, says that Krishna is always the *mat-prana-natak*—the Lord of His life. This holds true whether Krishna embraces Him tightly, or whether Krishna tramples Him or breaks His heart by not being present before Him. Once again, we are confronted with *sambhoga* and *vipralambha*—whether in union or in separation, Mahaprabhu remains true to the Lord of His life. This is the level of dedication required to reach the Supreme Destination.

In Shrimati Radharani's intense emotional state of divine love, Mahaprabhu calls Krishna a *lampatak*, or "a debauchee who mixes with other women." In other words, He is aware of Krishna's cunning nature. As the Supreme Personality, the independent Lord, Krishna can do whatever He likes, and the devotee is always aware of this. Such independence on Krishna's behalf increases the thrill of the relationship. Lord Krishna doesn't *have to* show His mercy—He may not. But, of course, He always does. This paradoxical wonder gives spiritual life its excitement.

This excitement is especially felt by the gopis of Vrindavan. The gopis, whose exemplary love is epitomized by Shrimati Radharani, will love Krishna no matter how Krishna treats them. Of course, Shri Krishna will not ultimately exploit them. That is the difference between material love and spiritual love. When such cart blanche fidelity manifests in this world, it is the worst kind of gullibility. One will be hurt and exploited, generally. But the gopis are spiritual, and they have totally dedicated their lives to Krishna, the Supreme Spirit.

Still, Krishna appeared to leave Vrindavan and, although He in actuality remained there in an unmanifest state, He went, by His plenary portion, Vasudeva, to Mathura. This served to put the gopis into a heart-rending state. "Would Krishna ever return?" they wondered. And they would cry out for Him: "Where has Krishna gone? Krishna! Krishna! Where are You?" So, you see, this brings us full circle: we are back to the chanting. This is the perfection of chanting, and our own chanting is meant to gradually evoke this remembrance: that we are looking for Krishna also. "Krishna—where are You?" This is our original refrain, too, and the chanting helps jar our memory. It helps us to become cured of our spiritual amnesia, as it were.

Anyway, due to their intense separation from Krishna, the gopis became broken-hearted, as Mahaprabhu commiserates in this verse, and they spent the rest of their lives feeling profound separation from Krishna. In that mood, in that separation, of course, they remembered Him constantly. This is technically called *lila-smaranam*, and it is very advanced. In this way, they associated with their dear Lord Krishna, experiencing *sambhoga* even in the midst of *vipralambha*. You follow?

In their separation, the gopis' love for Krishna did not diminish in the least, but it became even more intense. This is the purpose of love in separation, and this is why Krishna allows His devotees to go through this gut-wrenching yet transcendental experience. It increases their love. If a person is a pauper and then manages to accumulate some wealth—he really values it. What's more, if he then abruptly loses his wealth, he will think about it twenty-four hours a day. Similarly, in order to increase the love of His devotees, Krishna sometimes appears to be lost to them, and instead of forgetting Him, they feel that their transcendental loving sentiments increase.

This is real love. In spite of abuse, neglect, indifference, and all kinds of general mistreatment, the love goes on increasing. In this world, the closest thing to this phenomenon is perhaps a mother's love for her child. It is selfless, more or less. Of course, it is still material—so it is tinged. Love that is based on the body can never be totally pure. Therefore, when total submission and surrender manifests in this world, we feel a little suspicious; we can't understand it. And we're quite right. Here it is based on lust, not love, and it is only exploitation, without any spiritual underpinning. But in the relationship with Krishna and the gopis, it is only the *principle*, or the *mood*, of this phenomenon that we are talking about. The principle of total submission is there, but it lacks the unsavory characteristics of its material counterpart. So we are talking about the selfless conception of Absolute surrender and submission. It is quite different than the material counterpart, though, because in the ultimate analysis, Krishna is not our exploiter, but is, instead, our ever well-wisher. So it is spiritual. This is always to be remembered.

You see, when Mahaprabhu was in Puri, He was constantly absorbed in these feelings of the gopis, in separation from Krishna. And so He is personally teaching this worship of Krishna in separation, the highest kind of submission and love. Further, this teaching is being conveyed through the Lord's personal example, and also through His *Shikshashtakam* prayers, which have been recored in the *Chaitanya-charitamrita* and in Rupa Goswami's *Padyavali*, and in other places as well. The teaching is coming down through the other writings of the Goswamis, too. For the modern world, we are indebted to the lives and endeavors of Shrila Bhaktivinode Thakur, Bhaktisiddhanta Saraswati Thakur and, of course, we are mostly indebted to His Divine Grace A.C. Bhaktivedanta Swami Prabhupada, who took the eight prayers of Lord Chaitanya and distributed them to every town and village of the world.

(Originally published as a small booklet in 1990.)

WHERE THERE'S A CREATION
THERE IS A CREATOR

That every creation requires a creator was interestingly demonstrated by Sir Isaac Newton, the British scientist. Once he had a skilled mechanic make him a miniature replica of our solar system, with balls representing the planets geared together by cogs and belts so as to move in harmony when cranked. Later, Newton was visited by a scientist friend who did not believe in God. Their conversation is related in the *Minnesota Technologue* (October 1957): "One day, as Newton sat reading in his study with his mechanism on a large table near him, his infidel friend stepped in. Scientist that he was, he recognized at a glance what was before him. Stepping up to it, he slowly turned the crank, and with undisguised admiration watched the heavenly bodies all move in their relative speed in their orbits. Standing off a few feet he exclaimed, 'My! What an exquisite thing this is! Who made it?' Without looking up from his book, Newton answered, 'Nobody!'.

"Quickly turning to Newton, the infidel said, 'Evidently you did not understand my question. I asked who made this?' Looking up now, Newton solemnly assured him that nobody made it, but that the aggregation of matter had just happened to assume the form it was in—

and this is how the imitation solar system came to be.

"But the astonished infidel replied with some heat, 'You think that I am a fool! Of course somebody made it, and he is a genius, and I'd like to know who he is.'

"Laying his book aside, Newton arose and laid his hand on his friend's shoulder. 'This thing is but a puny imitation of a much grander system whose complex laws you know, and I am not able to convince you that this mere toy is without a designer and maker; yet you profess to believe that the original form from which the design is taken has come into being without either designer or maker! Now tell be by what sort of reasoning do you reach such an incongruous conclusion?"

Newton convinced his friend that whatever is made requires a maker—whatever is created requires a creator. If we but look about us in our daily lives, the same conclusion is forced upon us time and again. When you are in your room, ask yourself, "How much of this came about by evolution, and how much as the result of an intelligent creator?"

Did your desk evolve by chance or did it require a maker? What of your lamp, bed, chair, table, rug—or even the building itself? All these things required a maker! Even *you* had to have a mother and father! By what reasoning, then, can it be claimed that the most complex thing of all, living things, did not require a maker?

It was with good reason that Princeton University biology professor Edwin Conklin once said: "The probability of life originating from accident is comparable to the probability of the unabridged dictionary resulting from an explosion in a printing shop." (*Reader's Digest*, Jan. 1963, p. 92)

The assumption that life somehow spontaneously arises from matter is an antiquated philosophy surprisingly embraced, even still, by many material scientists. This entirely outmoded conception was once accepted by the ancient Greeks, too, who thought that living beings could be generated from mud and slime under the influence of heat. Although the concept of spontaneous generation was completely disproved in 1862 by a brilliant series of experiments performed before the French Academy by Louis Pasteur, modern biological science, in a feeble attempt to show the material origin of consciousness, has put forward the theory that living entities have evolved from primordial living creatures which have arisen by chance.

The "Bible" of this movement was Darwin's famous book, *The Origin of Species*. However, this book is now largely outdated for the very same reason that the present evolutionary theory will one day be outdated: it is simply based on mental speculation. As British scientist L.M. Davies once said: "It has been estimated that no less than 800 phrases in the subjunctive mood (such as 'Let us assume', 'Perhaps', 'It could be like this', etc.) can be found between the covers of Darwin's *The Origin of Species* alone." Seekers of genuine truth would do well to *bid adieu* to all speculative methods and instead conduct an avid study of the comprehensive and time-honored Vedic literature as presented in the *Journal of Vedic Heritage.*

(Originally published in *The Journal of Vedic Heritage*, No. 3, 1984)

12

ON HEARING

ew people recognize the true wonder of hearing. An article in the April, 1983 FDA Consumer describes the ear as a marvelous device which, when it's working right, "can hear sounds from all directions and, at the same time, maintain the body's equilibrium." When it's not working right, the consequences can be deafness, lack of balance, or both.

The ear is made of three parts. The outer ear captures and channels sound waves through the auditory canal to a tightly-stretched membrane known as the eardrum. Beyond this is the inner ear which contains three tiny bones. Sound waves on the eardrum cause these bones to vibrate. The vibration causes the bones to react in such a way that the sound message is conveyed to the inner ear.

The Eustachian Tube forms a tunnel from the middle ear to the back of the nasal cavity. It helps to drain the middle ear and permits pressure to equalize on both sides of the eardrum. It may also carry infections from the upper throat or tonsils to the middle ear. The inner ear has a number of fluid-filled chambers. Its lower portion ends in a delicate spiral structure shaped like a snail's shell. This is called the cochlea.

Just above the cochlea are three semicircular canals containing fluid.

These canals enable us to keep our balance when we sit, stand, walk, run or ride a bicycle. They also enable us to move forward or backward, up or down, etc., even with eyes closed. "The fluid in the canals and the hair-like nerve cells at the end of each U-shaped tube work something like a gyroscope, collecting information so the brain can tell the muscles what to do to maintain body balance," says the FDA article.

Clearly, the importance of the ear should not be minimized in any way. From hearing to walking (as in the problem of vertigo), the ear is indispensable.

So, too, is the ear indispensable in spiritual pursuits. Indeed, it has been said that hearing and chanting is the very means of liberation in our present day and age. In fact, it is sound vibration alone that can bring us to the highest level of spirituality, to love of God. This is confirmed in all of the world's most respected religious literatures. And of all sound vibrations, the Name of God is lauded as supreme.

This is only logical. God is supreme in every way. For instance, we may have some knowledge, but God has supreme knowledge. We may have some wealth, but God is the original proprietor of everything; He is the supreme proprietor and is thus supremely wealthy. In this way, God is supreme in all fields. He can only be described with superlatives. Thus, the revealed scriptures logically assert that God's name is supreme among names, and to hear God's name chanted is the supreme function of the ear; to chant His glories is the supreme function of the tongue.

Thus, King David preached, "From the rising of the Sun to its setting, the name of the Lord is to be praised" (*Psalms* 113:3). Later, Saint Paul taught, "Everyone who calls upon the name of the Lord will be saved" (*Romans*, 10:13). About six centuries after Paul, Mohammad counseled, "Glorify the name of your Lord, the most high" (*Koran* 87:2). Meanwhile, the tradition of achieving spiritual perfection through hearing and chanting was prevalent in India as well, where it was developed into a complex science. Some twenty-five hundred years ago, Buddha declared, "All who sincerely call upon My name will come to Me after death, and I will take them to Paradise" (*Vows of Amida Buddha*, 18). And thousands of years before that, the world's oldest religious literature, the Vedas, emphatically stated, "Chant the holy name, chant the holy name, chant the holy name of the Lord. In the Age of Kali there is no other way, no other way, no other way to attain spiritual enlightenment" (*Brhan-naradiya Purana*).

Understandably, different religions point to different names of God according to the language and cultural orientation of its origin. But the chanting of God's name is unequivocally recommended. Thus, we can understand that sound is of primary importance in both the material and spiritual worlds.

(Originally appeared in *The Whole Body Journal* [Special New Age Issue, Summer, 1985] and then in *Journal of Vedic Heritage*, No. 7, 1985)

TO KNOW GOD
IS TO LOVE HIM

The scene is a drive-in movie; it is late at night, and a young man is about to clumsily express his "love" for his newly found girlfriend. They had been introduced several hours earlier and, upon our young Casanova's request, the girl had agreed to meet him, have several drinks, and catch a movie at the local drive-in.

"What are you doing?" she asks suspiciously. Our enthusiastic friend nervously attempts to tell her what he thinks she'd like to hear: "I think I love you," he says. Incredulously, the girl responds to this all too familiar scene, "You *love* me?! You hardly even *know* me!!"

Love implies intimacy. We may chuckle at the above story, but let us give serious thought to the truths implied. The girl's point should be seriously considered—the boy, who hardly knew her, could not truly claim to love her; such "love" would certainly lack depth and meaning.

Love and knowledge of the beloved are inextricably related. The more you love someone, the more you want to get to know them; and unless you know someone, how can you actually claim to love them?

These same truths naturally exist on the spiritual platform. For instance, one of the most important biblical commentators of Medieval times,

Moses Maimonides, has written the following revealing statement in his *Mishna Torah*: "One can only love God through the knowledge one has of Him, and the love will be commensurate with the knowledge; when it is little, it will be little, and when it is much, it will be much. Therefore, a person must dedicate himself to pursue the disciplines of knowledge which reveal to him his Creator, to the extent that the human intellect is capable of comprehending it." (*Mishna Torah, Hilkhot Teshuvah* 10:1-6).

This is the statement of perhaps the most respected Jewish and biblical scholar of all time. Indeed, he was not only revered among Jews, but even St. Thomas Aquinas acknowledged him to be the most "profound knower of biblical truths."

Since knowledge of God can lead to love of God—and since love of God is admittedly the goal of all religious endeavors—then it logically follows that any tradition or body of literature that purports to have comprehensive and precise information in this regard is worth investigation, particularly if such a tradition and body of literature is time-tested and vouched-for by a plethora of saints and sages of the past (who have adhered to this tradition, studied this body of literature, and received the desired result). For these reasons we recommend the Vedic literature, the most lucid and exhaustive scriptural knowledge known to man.

The Vedic literature has been compared to an unabridged dictionary, while the other scriptures of the world have been compared to a pocket dictionary. The basic information is the same, but much more information is given in the unabridged dictionary. Analogically, this is quite appropriate. And when we let the scriptures speak for themselves, without a false notion of egalitarianism, it becomes clear just how appropriate this analogy is..

For example, Jesus has said, "There is much I have to tell you, but your ears are not ready to hear it yet." (Jn. 16:12) Similarly, Mohammed has said, "I have only spoken to men according to their mental capacities." (Arabic translation of the *Hadith* by Dr. M. Hafiz Syed)

Thus, by the admission of both Jesus and Mohammed, there was information about God that was not given to the followers of the Western religous tradition.

However, Lord Krishna says in the *Bhagavad-gita*, "I shall now declare unto you in full this knowledge both phenomenal and noumenal, by knowing which there will remain nothing further to be known." (B.G. 7:2) With a claim such as this, doesn't it make sense to take advantage of the information delivered within the Vedic tradition?

While the example of the young boy and girl at the beginning of this article may be trite and mundane, it nevertheless clearly illustrates the foolishness of the boy's position. How can you claim to love someone that you don't even really know? Those who are serious about developing their love for God would do well to make an in-depth study of the Vedic literature. Therein, one will find the most vast and nectarean information about the ultimate lovable object—Shri Krishna, the Supreme Personality of Godhead.

(Originally in *The Journal of Vedic Heritage*, No. 7, 1985)

OUR VEDIC HERITAGE

V edic culture is our birthright. This holds true not only for Hindus but for the rest of the world as well. This can be understood in light of the two following points, the first being exoteric, or external, and the second being more esoteric, or internal.

1) All cultures can be traced back to Vedic culture. For instance, it is believed by many anthropologists and social historians that many centuries ago there existed a land bridge across what is now the Bering Strait, connecting the Asian continent with the continent of North America. Many peoples of Eastern origin migrated across this land bridge into the area that we now call Alaska, gradually populating North and South America. This accounts for some of the striking similarities between, for example, the customs and cultures of the American Indians (including the South American Indians) and the Indian peoples of the Asian continent.

Similarly, we know that Buddhism, which is essentially a Vedic heterodoxy, had sent its missionaries to Western Persia by the second century before Christ; the basic teachings would easily have found its way through Syria to the sources of Christianity. To one who is familiar with the scriptures of the East (i.e.—*Bhagavad-gita, Upanishads*, etc.), there is no question that therein is found, at least in part, the primal origins of Occidental theology. And, finally, even such notables as the renowned historian Will Durant has called Vedic culture "the mother of civilization," while Toynbee has given his statement that the Vedic culture is at least six thousand years old (with an oral tradition that dates back still further). This would lead one to believe that it is the oldest literature known to man. Many say that it is. Thus, we all owe a great deal to Vedic culture—that culture from which all other cultures have sprouted forth.

2) Veda means "knowledge." And true knowledge is everybody's birthright. If truth is indeed true, it must be true everywhere and for everybody. It must transcend relative cultural orientations. The Vedic literature ultimately points in this direction. Thus, whether one considers himself a Hindu, Muslim, Jew, Christian, or whatever—Vedic knowledge is still his birthright, still his heritage. And one can use Vedic knowledge to be a better Hindu, Muslim, Jew, Christian, etc., because Vedic knowledge is indeed non-sectarian.

So we feel that a unification in the field of culture and knowledge is much desired, much needed. We feel that sectarianism has seen its day.

But this will be accomplished not by trying to force an external union between ideologies, or by eliminating from modern-day cultures all points of difference, thus leaving a weak residue, but by getting back to the esoteric basis of all cultures and by coming back to a sincere investigation of the common parentage of them all. In short, we must fully revive an awareness of the most ancient wisdom, the most profound heritage, our Vedic heritage.

(A short editorial for *The Journal of Vedic Heritage Anniversary Issue*, No. 8, 1985)

15

AYURVEDA: THE ORIGIN
OF HOLISTIC HEALING

Perhaps the oldest system of natural healing—predating even the Chinese system of medicine—is *Ayurveda*, a Sanskrit word which means "the knowledge of life" (*Veda*—Knowledge; *Ayu*—Life). A translation which more accurately reflects the scope of its subject, however, would be the "knowledge of longevity." This is so because the ancient sages of India were extremely careful to distinguish between *life*, a spiritual phenomenon, and *longevity*, a term which refers to the proper maintenance of the body.

Though freedom from death and disease has been the cherished goal in all ages, before one can search for immortality there must be a practical methodology for bodily maintenance. The achievement of these dual and interdependent goals is the purpose of Ayurveda. Thus, Ayurveda is more than just an ordinary medical science. It elucidates not only the healthiest interaction of the body and mind but also prescribes guidelines for realization of the relationship between body and mind to the eternal spirit within each of us. It is totally holistic.

While the science of Ayurveda was put into written form about

50 centuries ago, it has an oral tradition which dates back to antiquity. Meanwhile, over the millennia, several students of Ayurveda wrote voluminous encyclopedias—The *Charak Sambita* and the *Shushruta Sambita* (named after their respective authors)—which discussed in detail such subjects as pediatrics, obstetrics, gynecology, internal medicine, otolaryngology and plastic surgery. Modern scientists are still in awe at the depth and clarity of Ayurvedic information; it is a mystery that such a complex system was conceived so long ago.

The Tridosha Theory

An understanding of the Tridosha theory is central to an understanding of Ayurveda. The doshas are dynamic forces within the body and mind whose interactions produce the psychosomatic entity of a given person. The doshas are called Vata, Pitta, and Kapha—Sanskrit words that refer, respectively, to activity and motion, heat and energy, and structure and density. On the most gross platform, Vata, Pitta, and Kapha also refer to air, bile, and mucus. Through our daily activities, these forces are constantly moved into a state of disequilibrium—only to be cured by proper diet, climate, season, physical activity and mental discipline. Ayurveda deals with these things as a minute science.

Although genuine Ayurveda must be studied within a particular esoteric tradition, a good facsimile exists today and is actually quite common among the people of the Indian subcontinent. According to estimates made by the World Health Organization, there are over 500,000 practitioners of Ayurveda, a quarter of whom have training in recognized institutions during a five and one-half year period. Of 115 institutions where Ayurveda is taught, 98 offer training exclusively in Ayurveda and most are affiliated with major universities. Two hundred and thirty-nine hospitals and 15,000 dispensaries offer Ayurveda treatment throughout India.

If we study the history of Ayurveda, we have to go back to the Vedic period, as Ayurveda is believed to be *Upa Veda*, or a branch of Atharva Veda. In the Vedas—which are four in number (Rig, Sama, Yajur, and Atharva)—we find ample references to medicines, drugs, principles of treatment and descriptions of the different parts and organs of the body; thus the germ of Indian medicine no doubt lay in the Vedas, where, it is said, Ayurveda was originally espoused by Lord Dhanvantari (an incarnation of Vishnu). In fact, the Atharva Veda deals with this subject in great detail. We find therein not only the description of Dhanvantari and the cure for diseases, but the causes of diseases as well.

Interstingly, Ayurveda is comprised of eight branches, viz., (1) *Kaya* (general medicine), (2) *Shalya* (major surgery), (3) *Shalakya* (ear, nose, throat, mouth, and eye disease), (4) *Bhuta Vidhya* (psychiatrics), (5) *Kaumara Bhritya* (pediatrics), (6) *Agada* (toxicology), (7) *Rasayana* (rejuvenation or tonics), and (8) *Vajikarana* (virilification). Ayurveda elaborately discussed these things in the distant past. Indeed, India has many advanced secrets that are only now being discovered by Westerners.

This much historical background will be sufficient for the reader to see in Ayurveda the oldest medical system, and even if we ignore and omit the seemingly mythological elements, the existence of such advanced methodology—especially at a time when the world is generally thought of as being in darkness—should be sufficient to bring out the value of the Ayurveda system.

Historian Will Durant, in his famous work, *Our Oriental Heritage*, elucidates the unique nature of Ayurveda, and although the following is a long quote, it will give the reader a good idea of the distinguished scholar's opinion: "Appended to the Atharva Veda is the Ayurveda (The Science of Longevity). In this system of medicine, illness is attributed to disorder in one of the four humours (air, water, phlegm, and blood) and treatment is recommended with herbs and charms. Many of its diagnoses and cures are still used in India, with a success that is sometimes the envy of Western physicians. The Rig Veda names over a thousand such herbs and advocates water as the best cure for most diseases. Even in Vedic times, physicians and surgeons were being differentiated from magic doctors and were living in houses surrounded by gardens in which they cultivated medicinal plants.

"The great names in Hindu Medicine are those of Sushruta in the fifth century before and Charaka in the second century after Christ. Sushruta, Professor of Medicine in the University of Benares, wrote down in Sanskrit a system of diagnosis and therapy whose elements had descended to him from his tutor Dhanvantari. His book deals at length with surgery, obstetrics, diet, bathing, drugs, infant feeding, and hygiene and medical attention. Charaka composed a *Samhita* (or encyclopedia) of medicine which is still used in India and gave to his followers an almost Hippocratic conception of their calling: 'not for self, not for the fulfillment of any earthly desire of man, but solely for the good of suffering humanity should you treat your patients and so excel all.' Only less illustrious than these are the Vagbhata (625 A.D.) who prepared a medical compendium in prose and verse, and Bhava Misra (1550 A.D.) whose voluminous work on anatomy, physiology, and medicine mentioned, a hundred years before Harvey, the circulation of blood and prescribed mercury for that novel disease, syphilis, which had been recently brought in by the Portuguese as part of the Europeans' heritage to India.

"Sushruta described many surgical operations, cataract, hernia, lithotomy, Caesarian section, etc.—and 121 surgical instruments including lancets, sounds, forceps, catheters, and rectal and vaginal speculums. Despite Brahminical prohibitions, he described the dissection of dead bodies as indispensable in the training of surgeons. He was the first to graft upon a torn ear portions of skin taken from another part of the body, and from him and his Hindu ancestors rhinoplasty—the surgical reconstruction of the nose—descended into modern medicine.

"'The Ancient Hindus,' says Garrison, 'performed almost every major operation except ligation of the arteries. Limbs were amputated, abdominal sections were performed, fractures were set, hemorrhoids and fistulas were removed.' Sushruta laid down elaborate rules for preparing an operation and his suggestion that the wounded be sterilized by fumigation is one of the earliest known efforts of medicinal liquor to produce insensitivity to pain. In 927 A.D. two surgeons trepanned the skull of a Hindu king and made him insensitive to the operation by administering a drug called Samohini.

"For the treatment of the 1,120 diseases that he enumerated, Sushruta recommended diagnosis by inspection, palpation, and auscultation. Taking of the pulse was described in a treatise dating 1300 A.D. Urine analysis was described as a better diagnosis. Tibetan physicians were reputed able to cure any patient without having seen any more of him than his water. In the time of Yuan Chwang, Hindu medical treatment began with a seven day fast; in this interval the patient often recovered; if the illness continued, drugs were at last employed. Even then drugs were used sparingly; reliance was placed largely on diet, baths, enemas, inhalations, urethral and vaginal injections and blood lettings by leeches or cups. Hindu physicians were especially skilled in concocting antidotes for poisons. Vaccination, unknown in Europe before the eighteenth century, was known in India as early as 550 A.D., if we may judge from a text attributed to Dhanvantari."

How Ayurveda Works

The body is believed to be composed of five basic factors: *Prithvi* (earth), *Jala* (water), *Agni* (fire), *Akash* (ether), and *Vayu* (air). The whole universe is also believed to be composed of the same, and hence the food we eat, the water we drink, the air we breathe—all are composed of the same five chief components. This is the original idea— the foundation of Ayurvedic thinking— and it is supported by the harmony that exists between the microcosm and the macrocosm.

These five basic factors give rise to the three somatic doshas previously mentioned, *Vayu (vata)*, *Pitta*, and *Kapha*. According to these variables, Ayurveda teaches that persons should be treated differently, due to different types of physical constitution—a view which closely resembles that of many modern scientists. Accordingly, the three main physical constitutions are known as *Vatika*, *Paitika*, and *Kaphaja*. Ayurveda also adds that this physical constitution, being unchangeable, cannot be affected by medicine. Thus, Ayurveda is largely preventive.

The ancient sages have given in detail the particular physical as well as mental characteristics of each of these physical constitutions which can be found in any good book on Ayurveda.

There is a definite variation in the diet and habit of each physical constitution. However, there are other factors guiding the main response of the physical constitution of a person, such as race, country, seasons, hereditary factors, environment and so on.

Each physical constitution has got a different reaction to a particular drug or remedy, and hence an ideal Ayurvedic physician will never prescribe the same drug or medicine to everyone, but will make necessary changes in prescription, according to individuality, whereas modern medicine mainly aims at killing the germs or bacteria or the virus for destroying the infection.

Ayurveda thus defines "true" medicine, saying, "It is correct and pure medicine which cures a particular disease and doesn't give rise to other side reactions or diseases. It is the impure drug which temporarily cures the disease or supresses the symptoms and at the same time gives rise to other side reactions." The above principle, which evolved 3,000 years ago, is clearly understandable today, when many dangerous drugs and "remedies" cure and supress the particular symptoms in a miraculous way while they give rise to so many other side diseases.

Sometimes we may even see drugs that are more dangerous than the disease itself. This sort of danger is never present with the Ayurvedic treatment because the physician is not trying to treat the disease, but is trying to treat the patient as a whole.

Diet

Ayurveda generally prescribes a lacto-vegetarian diet—that is a vegetarian diet that includes dairy products. There are, however, other nutritional factors—and Ayurveda deals with them all. Nutrition refers to the nutritive substances found in food. We are accustomed to hearing about the calories, vitamins, minerals, carbohydrates and proteins that a particular food contains. But Ayurveda bases its nutritional science on a different set of measurements, the most important of these being the effects produced by the six *rasas*—sweet, sour, salty, hot, bitter, and astringent. These *rasas* refer to the foods' ultimate response in the body and not necessarily to how the foods taste. And although there are only six *rasas*, the combinations of these *rasas* are extensive. Just how and when one combines these various tastes will affect one's nutrition and one's overall health as well.

Recently, modern nutritional therapy has developed the use of large doses of vitamins and minerals synthesized from nature. But Ayurveda, for thousands of years, has taught the science of nutritional therapy without the need for expensive laboratories to turn out supplements. Different food combinations and simple herbs were prescribed in the Ayurvedic system and they worked just fine.

Unfortunately, this system has suffered much due to neglect, and there are few people who can apply it properly. But if one is fortunate enough to study Ayurveda under one who is an experienced practitioner—if one is ever treated by an Ayurvedic doctor—then one will feel very strongly about *bidding adieu* to modern allopathic medicinal techniques.

Balance

The balance of the doshas (and the good health that results from their balance) depends on moderation and regulation in eating and sleeping. This is cental to Ayurvedic treatment. When eating or sleeping is excessive, deficient or done at improper times or in an inappropriate way, there is every chance that all the doshas will become disturbed.

Excessive eating or sleeping is called *athi yoga*, and all of us have experienced to some degree its misery-producing effects. Deficient eating or sleeping is called *hena yoga*. When one artificially decreases his food or hours for resting the body, he invites a disturbance of the doshas that will lead to disease. Improper action in regard to bodily demands is called *mithya yoga*. Eating at the wrong time or in an unsuitable place are examples of this. Ayurveda recommends *sama yoga*—meeting bodily needs in a regulated and proper manner.

Proper eating must create a satisfied mind and a balanced feeling in the body. If the mind becomes agitated or dull or if the body becomes heavy and tired after taking food, that eating is improper. For proper eating, six factors should be considered: the place, the time of day, the duration of time since the last meal, the kind of foods to be eaten, the order in which the food should be eaten, and the person's state of mind.

Water before a meal is heavily recommended in Ayurveda. For one thing, obesity will be avoided. Appetite will be slackened. Water after a meal, it is said, leads to obesity and disease.

As far as eating goes, Ayurveda suggests taking sweets at the beginning of one's meals. Aside from the foods we normally taste as sweet, Ayurveda includes legumes and wheat in this category (Remember, Ayurveda judges by the ultimate reaction in the stomach—not by the way it tastes). These foods introduce body-building materials (such as amino acids) into the system. Modern science is also finding, after years of research, that such foods prepare the body for a meal and are most helpful at the beginning.

After the sweet-reacting foods are eaten, Ayurveda recommends the sour and salty foods. These foods consist of juicy, cooked vegetables, bean soup, and dairy (yogurt perhaps). They are basically liquid in character and increase the fire of digestion.

Then, some rice or solid food can be eaten—this will lead to a satisfying meal and will minimize one's chances of becoming ill. Ayurveda also recommends that bitter, hot or astringent foods be taken at the very beginning of a meal. Papaya, mango and yogurt aid in digestion. No strict follower of Ayurveda has ever complained about indigeston!

The basic rule, though, is that heavy—and especially sweet— foods should be taken at the beginning of the meal. This is because there is a greater secretion of hydrochloric acid in the stomach at this time. In the West we're accustomed to having our desserts last—thus we have a problem of obesity and indigestion (not to mention cancer and heart disease).

If a salad is eaten, Ayurveda suggests that it is taken with the sour or salty part of the meal. And the dressing should always have yogurt or lemon juice and salt. This makes the salad easier to digest and removes its tendency to increase the *vata* dosha (which produces distention of the abdomen, gas and constipation). Salads should not be eaten at the beginning of one's meals (as many people do) for the same reason.

Fruits, say the Ayurvedic texts, should not be eaten with a heavy meal. They should be eaten alone or with milk for a separate, light snack. Fruits are the equivalent of "candy" in Ayurvedic circles: the Ayurvedic diet will never become popular in a world of junk-food junkies!!

And while we're turning off those whose taste buds are already destroyed, we might as well mention that Ayurveda recommends a special food that when taken at the very end of a meal, will produce excellent health: fresh buttermilk. Buttermilk helps stimulate the digestive enzymes. It also replenishes the intestines with healthy flora (*acidophilus bacteria*) and maintains a proper acid-alkaline balance in the stomach. Don't worry, you can acquire a taste for it!

There are many variations on these themes, but this is a general overview of dietetics in Ayurveda. Personal tastes aside, the diet recommended by Ayurveda is the most nutritionally sound, even by today's standards. What's more, Ayurveda has literally hundreds of delicious, age-old recipes so an ardent follower doesn't get bored. Ayurveda offers a great deal to eat, a procedure for eating, and food for thought.

Daily Hygiene and Routine

A sound daily routine actually begins the night before sleep. Resting the body is necessary to bring the doshas into normal balance. Regulated sleep helps to prevent disease and loss of weight. It allows for the maximum formation of *virya*, the last-formed element in the body that gives one intelligence, determination and bodily luster. Irregular sleep will disturb the doshas, produce indigestion and make the limbs feel loose and disjoined from the body.

Sleeping during the day increases kapha dosha, and controls vata dosha. Excess sleep can cause mental disturbances, while sleeping at improper times can cause lack of appetite, feverishness, and headache. According to Ayurveda, sleeping during the day is allowed only when feeling ill or in the summer when the days are long. One may take a nap in the afternoon during this season.

Insomnia, the inability to fall asleep at the proper time, is due to an excess of vata dosha. To help alleviate this condition, the following program is recommended just before going to sleep:

(1) Massage the back of the head and soles of the feet with sesame oil.

(2) Put two or three drops of the oil in each ear.

(3) Take a warm bath.

(4) Drink a cup of warm milk with a half-teaspoon of tumeric.

When rising from bed after sleeping, one should stretch the body. This moves the doshas out from the center (heart region), where they stay during sleep, and it helps to activate the body. Ayurveda recommends that one try to defecate and urinate just after rising.

After defecation and washing, one may spray cold water over the face and eyelids and gargle with some cold water in the mouth. When the gums are hypersensitive, gargling with sesame oil is recommended. The teeth should then be cleaned with an astringent tooth powder (none of the American brands I know are astingent), or by chewing and brushing with the twig of a bitter or astingent tree. Nim and Babul trees are most recommended for this purpose, but any twig with the proper taste may be used.

Next, the tongue should be scraped with a gold, silver or copper scraper. The scraping removes accumulated mucus from the tongue, activates the body's lymphatic system and takes away foul odor from the mouth. The scraping should not be done too deeply, nor should the taste buds on the back of the tongue be scraped. The method is to stick the tongue out; the place on the tongue where it leaves the mouth is the place to begin scraping. Two or three strokes with the scraper are sufficient. For care of the throat, a gargle of warm water with a pinch of sea salt is recommended to help prevent throat disease and laryngitis, and to improve the quality of the voice.

The temperature of the morning bath or shower should begin with warm and end with cool. The cold should be as cold as the body can tolerate without producing shivering. Hot water should not be used; especially hot water should never be poured or sprayed over the head, as it will disturb *prana vayu*, the life air centered in the head.

Throughout the day, the natural urges of sneezing, crying, passing urine and stool, etc., should not be avoided. By artificially supressing them, the dosha will be disturbed and the *mala*, which is a waste product, will remain inside the body. On the other hand, one should not try to force these natural urges either.

The Ayurveda recommends morning exercise as part of a daily health routine. It says exercise increases one's energy and desire to work; it helps to regulate the fire of digestion, and it improves the metabolism (the conversion of one body element to the next). Before exercise, one should defecate if he has not yet done so that day. On the first day of exercise, one should go until he becomes exhausted. This allows him to see what is his present capacity. From there, he should do a minimal amount and gradually increase, day by day. *Yoga* exercises and *asanas* (postures) are the recommended activities for both the body and mind, along with quick walking. Strenuous exercise should not be done by one who suffers from a fever or a disease of the nervous system, or during the hot summer months. Kneading the muscles after exertion or exhaustion helps them to recover and eases pain.

After exercise, a massage may be taken. Massages can be given in two directions: from head to foot (away from the heart) and from foot to head (toward the heart). The former method (away from the heart) should be used for one who is slim or fatigued and for an infant. The latter method should be used for an obese or overweight person. Sesame oil is considered the best massage oil for the hot season; mustard oil for the cold season. Almond oil is especially good for massaging the head.

Massage should not be taken by a person with a fever or with diarrhea. It is also contra-indicated if there is swelling or infection. Massaging should never be done over the heart region. After a massage, a regular cold bath or shower should be taken, followed by some food.

Massage improves the complexion, blood vessels, and the circulation; it also tones muscles and exerts a soothing effect on the skin and nervous system. It improves vision, induces sleep and delays the aging process. An oil massage five or ten minutes before taking a bath is the best method for avoiding skin disease.

When time does not allow for a complete massage, a quick

routine of massage includes: the head, neck, spine, and soles of the feet. This can be done in less than five minutes as a self-treatment.

In the evening before taking rest, two or three drops of sesame oil should be dropped in each ear. This lubricates the middle ear and also helps to balance the *prana vayu* in the head. As previously mentioned, it is especially useful for those who have trouble falling asleep at night. It should be done as a daily routine. By keeping the opening to the senses cleansed in these ways, the doshas are also cleaned. External hygiene thus affects the internal balance and overall health of the body In this way, from morning to evening, Ayurveda prescribes simple procedures for the benefit of all. With the prevailing allopathic system, which generally seems to do more harm than good, Ayurveda should be a welcome relief, a friend for the body and soul.

(The article originally appeared in the January 1985 issue of *High Times*, a popular magazine published in the U.S.A.)

16

THE GITA AS IT WAS

A BOOK REVIEW OF *THE GITA AS IT WAS: REDISCOVERING THE ORIGINAL BHAGAVAD-GITA*, BY PHULGENDA SINHA (OPEN COURT, 1987)

The *Bhagavad-gita* ("The Song of the Supreme Lord") is one of the most important scriptures to come out of India. Although widely published and read as a separate text, *Bhagavad-gita* originally appears as an episode in the Mahabharata, a great historical epic consisting of some 100,000 Sanskrit couplets (The epic was recently popularized by Peter Brooks' nine-hour dramatization on stages around the world).

The *Gita* occupies chapters 25 through 42 in the *Bhishma Parva* section of the Mahabharata. As it begins, Lord Krishna is standing in the midst of a battlefield—as a charioteer—for His friend and devotee Arjuna. The dialogue that ensues is the *gita*, or "song," of *bhagavan*, "the Supreme Lord." He sings His song because His devotee, Arjuna, is in need of instruction.

Bewildered by the mandate to fight, Arjuna hesitates to engage in the fratricidal war before him. Lord Krishna, however, elucidates the implications of His devotee's reluctance. He points out that, as a warrior, Arjuna's specific duty was indeed to fight on behalf of the righteous. And his hesitation, though superficially noble, was actually based on illusion, a misidentification of the body with the self. The opposing party was, after all, guilty of many atrocities and already doomed, even if many of them were Arjuna's relatives. Krishna had already sealed their fate or, rather, they had sealed their own fate, and Krishna was merely encouraging Arjuna to act as His instrument in meting out the appropriate reaction. The *Gita's* 700 verses embody Lord Krishna's arguments in this regard and Arjuna's ultimate acquiescence.

What does this overview of the *Gita* have to do with Phulgenda Sinha's book? It appears that Arjuna's work was left unfinished. While he definitely did Krishna's work on the plains of Kurukshetra, there is a new enemy of his Lord's *Gita*—but this time the battlefield is academia and the weapon is independent research.

The *Gita* has been assaulted by unnecessary commentaries many times in the past, the earliest being the great Shankara commentary in the eighth century A.D. While important in its own right, it missed the essentially theistic nature of the *Gita's* overall message. Shankara's forced interpretation opened up a new school of philosophical hermeneutics for the *Gita*, and less worthy renditions soon flooded the market. Sinha lists them in his own work and doubtless refers to them as authorities: Aurobindo, Huxley, Hartmann, Steiner, Tagore, Schroder, Isherwood, to name a few. While these men may enjoy a certain distinction in their respective fields, they are hardly authorities on *Bhagavad-gita*.

The more important commentaries are hardly even mentioned by Sinha, but they should be known to our readers: The Anugita, The Gita-mahatmyas, Jayatirtha's commentary, the work of Vedanta Deshika, and even the more or less monistic interpretation of Bhaskara. More important still are the commentaries of Ramanujacharya, Madhvacharya, Vishvanath Chakravarti Thakur, and Baladeva Vidyabhushana; Sinha refers to them only superficially, for they do not support his view.

Interestingly, Sinha mentions every contemporary and popular edition of the *Gita*, with the conspicuous exception of *Bhagavad-gita As It Is* by His Divine Grace A.C. Bhaktivedanta Swami Prabhupada. And it is this definitive edition, it may be noted, that is ridiculed in the title of Sinha's work.

The premise of Sinha's book is not new. His obvious lack of respect for the traditional *Gita* (shown in the fact that he is ready to change its contents) is due to over 800 years of foreign influence in India—Muslim fundamentalists and Christian missionaries who denigrated the sacred scriptures of Indian antiquity. They had for centuries misled the Indian people, prejudicing them against their own culture, calling them barbaric and backward. The British, for instance, had convinced nearly the entire subcontintent that they were illiterate because they could not read English, and that they were irreligious because they did not know the Bible. These ill-informed foreigners had no idea of the highly sophisticated Sanskrit language or the comprehensive Vedic scriptural tradtion. Due to ignorance and cultural isolation, Indological study was held up for many centuries, and it still suffers from many of the early prejudices. Many modern academicians, for example, were and are weaned on this sort of misinformation. Sinha is clearly one of them.

His discovery of "the original *Gita*" is presented like a detailed detective mystery. Unfortunately, Sinha more resembles a bumbling Inspector Clouseau than a competent Sherlock Holmes. He cites authorities that were discredited years before his birth. And adding to the problem, he further cites Richard Garbe and even Weber, originators of "the Borrowing Theory," which states that all theistic notions found in the worship of Krishna are attributable to, or "borrowed" from Christianity. Sinha takes this notion even further, saying that there was no concept of a "One Almighty God" in India prior to the ninth century A.D.

What Sinha doesn't mention, however, is that these scholars who propounded the borrowing theory were eventually made the victims of their own misconceptions when the evidence of Megasthenes was brought in. This evidence engendered undeniable archeological conclusions, proving once and for all that Krishna worship is not only not derived from Christianity but that in fact it is the other way around. Moreover, the Megasthenes evidence made it clear that the worship of a "One Almighty God," as Sinha states it, was indeed accepted by early worshippers of Krishna—before the Christian Era (What to speak of the "ninth century A.D."!). The Megasthenes evidence is quite complex and beyond the scope of this short essay, but we can recommend that readers turn to this author's *Archeology and the Vaishnava Tradition: The Pre-Christian Roots of Krishna Worship* (Calcutta, KLM Firma, 1989) for more details.

Now let us get to the heart of Sinha's erroneous contention: All of the great commentators and the time-honored Vedic tradition are wrong! The *Gita* does not include 700 verses as is normally supposed. Rather, says Sinha, the original *Gita* is composed of a mere eighty-four and he kindly enumerates these carefully chosen verses in his book. But the problem is this: After going through this 250-page work more than four times, I still could not see exactly how he came to his conclusions. His evidence is poor; his clues are lacking. For anyone even moderately aware of Vedic culture, history, and theology, Sinha's detective mystery falls short of even a grade B movie.

In fact, his book lacks so much substance that a discerning reader might natually question if Sinha had possibly embarked upon his project to receive financial backing. Using ancient religious texts to obtain a grant for further research is not uncommon among modern academicians. According to a recent article in *India Abroad*, scholar Vedavyas (not to be confused with the compiler of the Vedic literature, who has the same name) discovered forty-five "missing" *Bhagavad-gita* verses. "The original text of the *Gita*," says Dr. Vedavyas, "had 745 verses, and now I will reveal the missing forty-five."

Hailed as an important scholarly breakthrough, Vedavyas' claim won him a grant and notoriety—for about two weeks. Then, in the same newspaper that acclaimed his discovery, came the startling counterclaim from another scholar, nullifying the forty-five-verse theory. And so it goes...

Almost as if in anticipation of such deviant interpretations, the *Gita* gives information as to how one can know the truths contained in its very pages. The fourth chapter sings loudly: *evam parampara praptam, imam rajarshayo vidhu.* This is the original Sanskrit, and it says, in essence, that one must approach a spiritual master in disciplic succession (*parampara*) to know the truth of the *Gita*; it will not suffice to apprach an academic research scholar. The mysteries of religious literature are best left to religious mystics, and scriptural hermeneutics are best left to those whose lives embody the scriptures. In this regard, the *Gita's* message is crystal clear: approach a self-realized soul. He can give you knowledge because he has seen the truth. By contrast, a mental speculator, however adept he may be, can only teach one how to speculate. One who studies *Bhagavad-gita* clinically—from a distance—can never enter into its deeper understanding. One who *lives* the *Gita*, however, can resolve all philsophical, historical, and hermeneutical problems, both for himself and for those he teaches.

Sinha is in the former category. His approach is academic, speculative. And it is a poor academic and speculative approach at that. Not detective-like, but defective-like. Sinha's publishers, Open Court, have published other, more worthy *Gita*-type books for scholars and laymen alike. *The Universal Gita* by Eric J. Sharpe was Open Court's first attempt in this area. This delightful book gives an accurate view of the story behind the *Gita* and documents its journey West. The reader is introduced to important Western Transcendentalists who found more than a little merit in the *Gita's* teaching: T.S. Eliot, R.W. Emerson, H.D. Thoreau, Walt Whitman, and even Albert Einstein are included.

After the success of *The Universal Gita* in 1985, Open Court released an even more ambitious work: Arvind Sharma's *The Hindu Gita.* This scholarly book picked up where Sharpe's book left off, detailing the traditional Indian commentaries from Shankara to Madhva. Sinha could have greatly benefited from reading these two books. Since *The Hindu Gita* did as well for Open Court in 1986 as *The Universal Gita* did the year before, the logical conclusion was to keep the *Gita* material coming. Unfortunately, they took too big a risk with Sinha's work. Scholar's reject it as lacking evidence. Believers denounce it as untraditional and sacrilegious. I just felt it was a waste of paper.

(This book review originally appeared in *Clarion Call Magazine*, Vol. 2, No. 2, 1989.)

THE GLORIES OF LORD RAMA

he chanting of "Hare Krishna" is now a colorful, familiar sight on the streets of most major cities—"*Hare Krishna, Hare Krishna, Krishna Krishna, Hare Hare/Hare Rama, Hare Rama, Rama Rama, Hare Hare.*" Few people are aware, however, of the literal translation: "O Lord. O Energy of the Lord. Please engage me in Your service." This chant is considered eternal, and it is directly imported from the spiritual world. In India, it is known as the *maha-mantra*, the greatest of all prayers.

According to ancient India's Vedic literature, the name "Krishna" denotes the Supreme Personality of Godhead, the source of all incarnations. It refers to God beyond opulence and majesty—His manifestation as the pinnacle of loving exchange. Thus its appearance in the *maha-mantra* is natural and to be expected. The greatest name for the greatest prayer.

But the appearance of the name "Rama" is a bit different. Although it is certainly a name for God, it does not necessarily denote the *supreme* manifestation of the Lord, but a secondary one. Out of an unlimited variety of names for the Supreme Being, why does the name "Rama" appear in the *maha-mantra*? What is the special significance of this particular manifestation of God? Although, in one sense, the names of God as they appear in the *maha-mantra* cannot be questioned (being eternal and absolute), in this article we will examine the unique position of Lord Rama.

God has an unlimited variety of names. In the Bible and Koran, for instance, God is popularly known as Jehovah and Allah. But both scriptures enunciate other names of God as well. And in the Vedic literature, a veritable storehouse of names and incarnations of God are described. So, why—out of all these names—is "Rama" used in the *maha-mantra*, the greatest prayer?

It should be noted that in the *maha-mantra* Rama refers, chiefly, to *Radha-raman-rama*, or "Krishna who loves Radha." But the word *Rama*, in that same *mantra*, more commonly refers to two different Personalities of Godhead. Rama can mean Balaram, Lord Krishna's first and most immediate expansion, or Rama can refer to Lord Ramachandra, an incarnation of Krishna Who graced this earth millennia ago. In the *maha-mantra*, both "Ramas" are evoked.

Since Balaram is so intimately connected with Krishna—theologically and no less in His manifest pastimes—His name is easily understandable as a candidate for inclusion in the *maha-mantra*. Being Krishna's most immediate expansion, He is certainly worthy of glorification in the greatest of all prayers. It is said that the only difference between Krishna and Balaram is the color of Their complexion.

But Lord Ramachandra's story is different. He is but one of the unlimited incarnations of God mentioned in the Vedic literature. His incarnation must indeed stand out to be given the distinction of appearing in the *maha-mantra*.

In fact, Lord Ramachandra is one of the most popular manifestations of God in all of India. When the average Indian chants "Hare Rama" of "He Rama," as Mahatma Gandhi did when his life came to an end, he is generally referring to the greenish-hued incarnation Lord Rama.

The word *Rama* means "the all-pleasing one," and it indicates that all pleasure ultimately comes from God. The story of Lord Ramachandra has indeed brought pleasure to all who have been fortunate enough to hear it. And because it focuses on an incarnation of the Lord, hearing it is purifying and enlightening as well.

The Ramayana

The pastimes of Lord Ramachandra are narrated in the *Ramayana*, a

Vedic text which predates the Bible by thousands of years. In India, the adventures of Lord Rama are studied by scholars, enjoyed by laymen and taught to children. The *Ramayana* is a national favorite, and has been so for uncountable generations.

It has seven long sections called *kandas*. The first, *Bala-kanda*, tells us of Rama's appearance into this world. According to *Bhagavad-gita*, India's unexcelled treatise on metaphysics, understanding the mysterious nature of the Lord's appearance and activities qualifies one for entering the spiritual realm. This is no easy task. Literature such as the *Ramayana* is helpful.

The word *Bala* refers to the Lord's "childhood" or "youthful" pastimes. And the *Bala-kanda* thus takes us from Lord Rama's birth, through His childhood and youthful pastimes, and finally ends with His marriage to Princess Sita (the Goddess of Fortune).

The second section of the *Ramayana, Ayodhya-kanda*, introduces the intrigue at Ayodhya, the magnificent city/kingdom ruled by King Dasarath, Rama's father in this mortal world. The kingdom is offered to Rama, but a complex series of events prevents Him from obtaining it. And He is banished to the forest instead. His faithful wife Sita, and Laksman, His brother (the Lord's expansion), go with Him.

Next, *Aranya-kanda*, deals with Their adventures in the wilderness (*aranya*). In exotic and exciting trappings, such as the Dandaka Forest, the Pancavati Glade, and the Kraunca Jungle, the Divine Trio spend about twelve years, knowing both intense happiness and terrible misfortune. The people of India have utilized the truths implied in these stories to deal with their own pleasure and pain. The *Ramayana* teaches them to take the fortunes of life as the Lord's mercy—and the tribulations as a test of devotion, a test of love. We see Princess Sita's test, as She is kidnapped by the evil Ravana—but She remains true to Rama. This teaches us that we, too, should remain true to God, steadfast in our devotion, despite any and all setbacks. And the *Aranya-kanda* explains this with beautiful metaphor and compelling drama.

The plot develops into an exciting array of mini-adventures, as we enter the *Kishkindha-kanda*. Here, Rama joins forces with Sugriva and Hanuman (monkey warriors) in an attempt to find Sita. Then, section five, known as *Sundara-kanda*, shows the glory of Hanuman, the embodiment of devotion, as he finds Sita and delivers to Her a message from Rama. Her rescue is near. This section is beautifully written and enchants its readers with confidential details of loving exchange.

The *Yuddha-kanda*, or the sixth section of the *Ramayana*, tells of the heart-rending meeting of Rama and His arch-enemy Ravana. Included is a detailed description of their final battle. This is important because it shows the inevitable mastery of good over evil, and further, of the spiritual over the material.

Yuddha means "war." And this section graphically outlines a devastating battle—with thousands of warriors—culminating in the freedom of Sita and the death of Ravana. It is the longest and yet most popular part of the *Ramayana*, and it is replete with heroism, chivalry, and spiritual instruction. The *Yuddha-kanda* ends with the return of Lord Rama and Sita to Ayodhya, Their triumphant return being ushered in by thousands of citizens holding bright candles—victorious flames— in Their honor. The coronation is festive and heart-warming.

The last of the seven sections is called *Uttara-kanda*. According to all Vedic scholars, the most important teaching here is Sita's faithfulness to Rama (and vice versa), despite Her time spent with Ravana. Fidelity is a primary theme throughout the *Ramayana* and it reaches its zenith in the expression of love between Rama and Sita, especially in *Uttara-kanda*.

And despite Their love for each other, Rama tests Sita's chastity, not because He doubts Her, but, as an exemplary king, He must be considered beyond reproach. And so should Sita. Thus the *Ramayana* ends not only with a lesson in love and fidelity, but with a lesson on how to do one's duty perfectly. This was exemplified in the Personality of Rama, Who set the example of a model husband, a superlative administrator, and a well-wisher of every living entity.

The Rama Motif

Although the *Ramayana* is a very long story of 24,000 couplets, the above will serve as a general outline. Being anxious for the eternal truths found in its verses, many differrent cultures have imported more than just an outline of the *Ramayana* to their shores.

In China, for instance, famous folk tales about "the Wind Monkey" are obvious take-offs on the pastimes of Hanuman, Lord Rama's great devotee. And down through the ages all of China has marveled at the series of adventures this fabulous "monkey" goes through.

As the *Ramayana* was transported to Thailand, its title was transposed to *Ramakiyan*, but it is basically the same story, with few changes. It is still one of the most popular stories in that country.

Elements from the Rama motif are used in two Buddhist stories, and the Jains have utilized the *Ramayana* to inculcate their own religious values as well. Drawing on the rich heritage of Vedic knowledge, the Jains would retell the story of Rama, pointing out the valuable lessons in morality and ethics which it clearly enunciates.

Much later, the Sikhs embraced the Rama-story as their own and considered the Personality of Rama as the emblem of righteousness. The tenth Sikh guru, Govinda Singh (1666-1708), wrote no less than 860 short volumes about the prince of Ayodhya.

It is noteworthy that so many different cultures and religious milieus find the Ramayana spiritually important. It is one of the only stories (if not the only story...) of a particular manifestation of God to be embraced by such a wide variety of peoples.

In fact, the story of Rama is so important that it is reiterated many times in other parts of the Vedic literature. While the *Ramayana* gives us the full account of Lord Ramachandra's exploits, the mysteries of His descent are explained elsewhere, in capsulated form.

In the *Mahabharata's* third book, for instance, the *Aranyaka-parva*, there is a nineteen chapter summation of the story of Rama. Known as the *Ramopakhyana*, this section appears right after Draupadi has been recovered after a long trial of separation. The sage Markandeya likens the situation to the abduction of Sita, and he elaborates on the events which led to Her eventual rescue. Thus, the implications of the Rama motif are used in the *Mahabharata*.

Likewise, there are seven *puranas* which again reiterate the importance of the *Ramayana*. In alphabetical order, they are the *Agni-purana, Bhagavat-purana, Brahmavaivarta-purana, Garuda-purana, Kurma-purna, Shiva-purana, and the Vishnu-purana*.

Included in these is the *Bhagavat-purana*, also known as the *Shrimad Bhagavatam*, the ripened fruit of the Vedic tree of knowledge. This is significant, for the *Bhagavatam* only deals with the essence of spiritual wisdom.

When the compiler of the Vedic literature, Vyasadeva, put the Vedas into written form some five thousand years ago, he felt despondent. His spiritual master then informed him that his despondency was due to the fact that he had neglected, in all of his previous writings, to describe the all-important name, fame, form, and pastimes of the Supreme Personality of Godhead. Vyasadeva thus compiled the essence of Vedic knowledge in the *Shrimad-Bhagavatam.* The story of Rama is included therein.

Conclusion

The incarnation of Ramachandra is thus established as important. Of course, all incarnations and manifestations of God are important. Being spiritual, They are all on the self-same Absolute platform. Still, there *is* spiritual variegatedness, and among the unlimited manifestations of God, Ramachandra enjoys a special position, even in the fact that His name appears in the *maha-mantra.*

Today, India's equivalent of New Year's Day is called Diwali, a national holiday, and it commemorates the welcoming of Rama back to Ayodhya. As they lit candles then, so they continue, every year, as Diwali is celebrated. The words of the *Ramayana* ring true: "So long as mountains and rivers have a place on earth, the story of Rama will be adored in the universe." Love for the Personality of Rama continues to this day. Some say that this love can be traced to Rama's humanity, for unlike many other incarnations of God, Rama gave us a life-story that we can use as a prototype for our own. Whatever the reason, Rama is a specifically significant incarnation, and He is loved throughout the world.

Thus the *maha-mantra* glorifies this great manifestation of the Supreme—*Hare Krishna, Hare Krishna, Krishna Krishna, Hare Hare/Hare Rama, Hare Rama, Rama Rama, Hare Hare.* And the scriptures tell us: "As far as the holy names of Rama and Krishna are concerned, They are on an equal level, but for further advancement we require some specific information from revealed scriptures...The holy name of Ramachandra is equal to one thousand holy names of Lord Vishnu...The pious results derived from chanting the thousand holy names of Vishnu three times can be attained by only one repetition of the holy name of Krishna." (*Brahmanda-purana.* Also cited in *Chaitanya Charitamrita, Madhya-lila,* chapter 9, verses 31-33)

The great Vedic teachers have thus concluded that for every three times one chants the name of Rama, one can attain the same results by chanting the name of Krishna once. And if one dedicates himself to the chanting of the Hare Krishna *maha-mantra*—which includes both Rama and Krishna—one will surely develop love of God in due course.

(Originally published in ISKCON New York's monthly newsletter, *On the Way to Krishna* [Special Rama issue] in the winter of 1985)

18

K R I S H N A :
T H E   P E R F E C T
N A M E   O F   G O D

Krishna is a name for God. It means "the All-Attractive One." God, of course, is known by hundreds and millions of names. Some of them—Jehovah, Adonai, Buddha, and Allah—are familiar to us, while the name Krishna may be less so. However, Krishna *is* a name for God and, in many ways, it is His most appropriate name.

Some people feel that God has no name. A name would be limiting, such people think, and God is limitless by definition.

Although it is certainly true that God is unlimited, this in no way disqualifies Him from having a name. It may be true that no name can do Him justice, and in this sense He has no name. But, in another sense, God has unlimited names to describe his limitless attributes. If one were to call God "the Unlimited One," as many do, would *that* name be limiting? Of course not. In a similar fashion, God has an endless variety of names, and they all describe different features of His Absolute Personality.

God's names are themselves Absolute, and anyone who chants them will derive spiritual purification from doing so. Chanting God's name is the same as associating with Him. This is because God is Absolute, beyond duality. If there was a difference between God and His name (just as in the material world—a thing and its name are two different things), that would create a sense of duality—there would be two separate things: God and His name. Thus, God must be fully present in His name—they must be intrinsically the same thing; in this way He is beyond duality; He and His name are one.

Still, certain names are more appropriate than others when describing the Supreme Personality of Godhead. The word *God*, for instance, which is of Germanic origin, simply refers to "the Good One."[1] God is certainly "good." In fact, He is supremely Good. But we must admit that the appellation *God* is far from being a descriptive name of the Supreme Being; it is insufficient. There are other names which are more accurately characteristic of His Supreme Nature. Actually, English is a rather poor language for communicating theological subjects.

In the Bible, the word that is usually translated as "God" is the Hebrew *Elohim*. It can be broken down further to *El*, which means "mighty, strong, prominent."[2] Still, it falls short of an actual description of the Supreme Being. The other names for God in the Bible—El-Shaddai[3], Adonai[4], Jehovah[5]—mean basically the same thing; they indicate God's Lordship, His majesty. And we indeed see that the side of God the Bible reveals is His mighty, fearful, and powerful side.

But there is more to God than this. And in the New Testament, Lord Jesus Christ actually shows us another side of God, a side that is more personal and loving. Indeed, Jesus referred to God in Aramaic, as *Awoon*, or "our Universal Father." Jesus accentuated God's Fatherhood and the concomitant fact that we are all His children.

Examining the Islamic names for God, we find the Arabic term *Allah*, which many scholars have translated as "He who gives life,"[6] indicating that all life comes from God and that we are all brothers under His sovereignty. Thus, the name Allah is similar to Jesus' Awoon.

---

1 Rocco A. Errico, *The Ancient Aramaic Prayer of Jesus*, (Los Angeles, CA., Science of Mind Pub., 1978).
2. Nathan Stone, *Names of God*, (N.Y., Moody Press, 1944).
3. Ibid.
4. Ibid.
5 It should be noted here that the Hebrew Bible uses the Tetragrammaton YHWH most frequently of all the names for God. Christian theologians, who had an inadequate knowledge of Hebrew pronunciation and vowel-phonics, substituted for it, beginning with the year 1518, a form of Yahveh; namely Jehovah. But this name is considered inaccurate by Hebraic scholars (see *The Book of Jewish Knowledge* by Nathaniel Ausubel, Crown Publishers, 1964).
6. Isa Mohamad, *Why Allah Should Not Be Called "God"* (N.Y., Ansaru Allah Pub., 1979).

In India, there are literally millions of names for God. And ancient India's Vedic literature, which was compiled in Sanskrit, delivers the most descriptive words for Him. In fact, the Vedic literature and the entire Sanskrit lexicon was conceived for this purpose—to give all of mankind exacting, detailed information about the Supreme Personality of Godhead.

The Sanskrit word *Buddha* refers to "the Enlightened One," and, when used in connection with God, indicates that He is supremely enlightened. The name Govinda, another Sanskrit name, indicates that all pleasure comes from God. He gives pleasure to the senses, the saintly persons, and to the cow. Similarly, the name Rama connotes the reservoir of all pleasure. And the Sanskrit name Adhokshaja refers to the fact that God is beyond the purview of the senses. He is beyond experimental knowledge. In this way, the Vedic literature reveals a great variety of names for God; and all these names are meant to give us a greater understanding of His nature.

But God must be complete to be God—He must be full in all opulences. Some people may be attracted to His Goodness, or even His majestic aspect—His might and power—as it is revealed in the Old Testament. Still, others may not. Some may be attracted to the "Fatherly" aspect that Jesus accentuated to his followers. Some may not be attracted by this aspect. The fact that God is beyond the purview of the senses and that He is "the giver of life"—the Islamic aspect—this may appeal to a certain class of people. But not to all. Or God's "All-intelligent" feature—the fact that He's naturally enlightened—this will also attract some.

But there are people who are not attracted to the intellect, to elusiveness, to Fatherhood, to power. The names of God that connote the above characteristics will only attract people who are already attracted to those qualities, either consciously or unconsciously. God, however, is the reservoir of all supreme qualities, and the name that connotes this would be necessarily more complete than all the rest.

One who is attracted by knowledge may not be attracted by power. Thus, the names Adonai, El-Shaddai, and Jehovah—the names that refer to God's majesty and Lordship—will not suffice for such a person, for they reveal only an aspect of God's glory. Similarly, one who is attracted by power and might, may not be attracted by knowledge. Such a person will obviously find the Buddha concept lacking. And so on, for all of the above names.

The name Krishna, however, indicates one who is All-Attractive. To be all-attractive, one must have complete strength, beauty, wealth, fame, knowledge and renunciation. Thus, the name Krishna is all-inclusive. Krishna is therefore also known as *Bhagavan*, indicating that He is complete in all of these opulences.

So the names of God with which we are familiar reveal but an aspect of His greatness, while the name Krishna, with which we may be less familiar, indicates God in all His glory, with no opulence lacking. This, indeed, is the name of God par excellence.

Now, one may wonder, if the name of Krishna is supreme, why was it not revealed by the prophets of Biblical times? If the concept of Krishna is higher, why did Jesus not reveal it to his followers?

The Vedic literature states that a God-realized person reveals truths about God according to the time, place, and circumstance, according to the mental and devotional capacity of his audience. In the Biblical times, for instance, Jesus had to tell his followers "thou shalt not kill" and similar instructions; obviously, he was preaching to persons who he thought might require such a fundamental commandment. Similarly, Mohammed had to teach his followers not to have sex with their mothers. There is actually such a commandment in the Koran. Clearly, he was preaching to less than spiritually-advanced people. Actually in Arabia, at the time Mohammed appeared, there were no religious principles at all. Many were burying their children alive, unnecessarily keeping more than one wife, and spending the day in a drunken stupor. This was the culture in which Mohammed had to deliver the Koran.

But the Vedic literature was revealed to the greatest among sages. This accounts for the intensity of the subject-matter and the depth of the spiritual revelation. The Vedas are able to deal with spirituality as a complex science, while other scriptures of the world are largely confined to ethical codes and moral principles. Accordingly, the Vedas reveal very elaborate concepts and names of God, the likes of which are unknown in other religious literatures. However, all religious literature is meant for the gradual upliftment of society in general. To this end, religious truth is revealed selectively, according to a given culture's secondary characteristics. Primary characteristics—essential human traits—are the same everywhere. But secondary characteristics vary according to cultural conditioning.

Although human nature is the same everywhere, people living in different nations and on different continents acquire different secondary characteristics. It is impossible to find two people living in the world who have exactly the same secondary nature. Even two brothers born from the same womb will differ in appearance and personality, what to speak of people born in separate countries. In different regions, things such as the locations of bodies of water, air currents, mountains and forests, and the availability of foodstuffs and clothing all vary. Consequently, differences naturally occur in people's appearance, social status, occupation, and style of dressing and eating. Each nationality has a particular disposition of mind, and thus of various conceptions of the Supreme Lord. While it may be the same in essence, it may appear superficially dissimilar. As people in different places rise above their aboriginal condition and gradually develop culture, science, law, and devotion to God, their means of worship also diverge in terms of language, costume, kinds of offerings, and mental attitudes. However, when we impartially consider all these secondary characteristics we find no discrepancy. As long as the object of worship is the same, it does not detract from the authenticity of their religion. Therefore Lord Chaitanya has specifically ordered that we should execute our own service to the Supreme Lord in the mode of pure goodness and at the same time refrain from ridiculing the codes of others.

Under the influence of the above factors, the religious systems proclaimed by different nationalities vary in the following ways:
(1) different spiritual masters;
(2) differences in mental and emotional attitudes towards worship;
(3) different prescribed rituals of worship;
(4) different types of affection for and activities in relation to the object of worship;
(5) different names and terminologies resulting from differences in languages.

When we think about it, it becomes obvious that spiritual revelation is given in a language which is suitable for people in a certain locality. We sometimes forget that Jesus, for instance, never used words like "God," "Lord," and the many other names we use today. Jesus didn't speak English—he spoke Aramaic! And yet some will criticize Hare Krishna devotees for using names of God that Jesus and the prophets never used. If they can use the word "God" for the Supreme Being, which, again, Jesus never uttered, we can certainly use the word "Krishna."

Etymologically, the word *Hebrew* indicates a people who have "crossed over." Generally, it is taken to refer to the people who have "crossed over idolatry into the worship of the One God." Thus, any person who worships One Supreme God—as opposed to many gods—

may, in a sense, be deemed "a Hebrew." Further, the word *Jew*, which is derived from Judah, merely implies that these people "exalt the Lord." Once again from a strictly philological point of view, anyone who exalts the Lord may be called "a Jew." Of course, these words have come to mean something else, describing a whole ethnic and religious culture. But originally there were no such distinctions between lovers of the Lord. One can consider the word *Islam*, as well. *Islam* means "submission to the will of God." One who does the submitting is called a Muslim. In this way, the names of the various religious processes throughout the world indicate a more universal application, a non-sectarian form of religion.

Because of the variety of spiritual authorities, in some places people honor the Vedic sages, in others they revere the prophets led by Mohammed, and in still other regions they esteem the religious personalities who follow Jesus. Similarly, in each locality many different men of knowledge are shown particular respect. Each community should, of course, properly honor its own spiritual masters, but simply for the sake of gaining followers, no one should try to establish that the instructions given by one's own local spiritual master are better than the instructions of spiritual masters everywhere else. The propagation of such an antagonistic position would certainly be inauspicious for the world. Rather, in an unbiased way, one should observe religious processes, and give credit where credit is due. Hopefully, the sincere will embrace as their own the process that reveals God the most (and not fall victim to foolish prejudices).

Pure, unalloyed love of God is the actual religion of the spirit soul. Thus, in spite of the five kinds of distinctions among religious systems, mentioned above, we should recognize as genuine any religious process whose goal is the realization of pure love of God. It is useless to quarrel over superficial differences. If the goal of a process is pure, then the system is fully auspicious.

However, whatever name of God or process we may accept, all scriptures enjoin us to chant these names for spiritual purification. This is the recommended process of self-realization for the present age.

Mohammed counseled, "Glorify the name of your Lord, the most high." (*Koran* 87.2); Saint Paul said, "Everyone who calls upon the name of the Lord will be saved" (*Romans* 10:13); Lord Buddha declared, "All who sincerely call upon my name will come to me after death, and I will take them to Paradise." (*Vows of Amida Buddha* 18); King David preached, "From the rising of the sun to its setting, the name of the Lord is to be praised." (*Psalms* 113:3); And the world's oldest scriptures, the Vedas of India, emphatically state, "Chant the holy name, chant the holy name, chant the holy name of the Lord. In this age of quarrel there is no other way, no other way, no other way to attain spiritual enlightenment." (*Brhan-naradiya Purana*).

The chanting of Krishna's name has been going on in India for thousands upon thousands of years. This is documented in the Vedic literature. And even today, millions of people, both in India and around the world, chant "Hare Krishna" for spiritual fulfillment.

The special design of the Hare Krishna chant makes it easy to repeat and pleasant to hear. Spoken or sung, by yourself or in a group, Hare Krishna invariably brings us back to our primordial state of spiritual awareness—Krishna consciousness. This is the power of the name of Krishna.

(This essay was printed as a tract and distributed throughout North America.)

FEMINISM AND THE
QUEST FOR GOD

The feminist movement was bound to be successful, at least to some degree. After all, the basic premises of feminism are certainly reasonable. Why should a woman be paid less than a man for doing the same job? Or why should any position be denied to a qualified woman simply because she is a woman? In this sense, feminism is a pragmatic social movement and in no way conflicts with the principles of spirituality. Still, there is an entirely different dimension to feminism that brings it into sharp conflict with most of the world's major religious traditions.

Feminism in the United States was first recognized at the turn of the century when the suffragettes demonstrated for, and ultimately won, the right to vote. During the past two decades the tide of resurgent feminism has become an almost irresistible force, sweeping aside barriers as old as society itself.

Today, women are heavily represented in most professions and businesses. Women serve in both houses of Congress, in the Cabinet, and on the Supreme Court and at all levels of government branches. As of writing this article, they are seriously being considered for the vice presidential nomination by both major parties in the United States.

To a large degree, however, modern feminism has become extremist, and now it addresses issues that are far beyond its scope. Thus, abortion becomes a feminist issue because it involves the right of a woman to "control" her own body. Nevermind that she is taking a life. Nevermind that she is "controlling" someone else's body. Or take religion, for instance. Does feminism apply? These are human issues, and they affect each and every living entity, regardless of gender.

Even Germaine Greer, the buoyant, well-known feminist leader, has recently changed her point of view, going so far as to endorse "motherhood" as the ultimate career. Striding through the exotic streets of India, Greer found it refreshing to see the women working in the fields alongside their husbands, without "the aberrant whine of the frustrated career wife anywhere in sight."

Ms. Greer's latest book, *Sex And Destiny*, may mark the finish of her feminist leanings. In fact, the book makes it clear that she now appreciates the noble, simple women of Third World countries, and she aspires for their spiritual insight as well. The purpose of life should be pursued by all individuals, feminist or not. In whatever way a proponent of women's rights may choose to approach this, one thing is certain: many women are experiencing a profound dissatisfaction with the role of the woman and the way she is perceived by herself and society.

There may very well be ample justification for the dissatisfaction of the feminists. Perhaps they have indeed been oppressed and exploited by a male-dominated society. Let us not forget, however, that it is a *materialistic* society in which this entire scenario is taking place. Exploitation is a symptom of selfishness. Selfishness is a symptom of the bodily concept of life. And the bodily concept of life is at the heart of materialistic thinking. If one identifies himself (or herself!) as nothing more than a material body, the body becomes of central interest—more important than the person within. Bodily differences are accentuated. Spiritual unity is overlooked. It would seem that the solution to exploitation—the major problem facing the feminists—is to obliterate materialism, not sexism. Sexist thinking is a symptom of the disease—the disease is materialism.

Viewed superficially, the world's great religious traditions are quite an inviting target for feminism, and they have indeed come under attack. Do the world's major religious scriptures claim that women are inferior? If so, does this alleged inferiority give way to exploitation?

First of all, God is obviously unbiased. All religious scriptures show case histories of women who have attained the perfection of spirituality. Ancient India's *Bhagavad-gita* boldly announces that "...women can attain the Supreme Destination." (Bg. 9:32)

Further, we must draw a clear distinction between the difficulties of the secular feminist and the woman who adheres to a life of spirituality. The secular feminist faces not only exploitation and oppression, but also an artificial barrier erected by the male members of society. It is the strength of the male as opposed to that of the female that keeps this barrier intact. As women become more militant and men more conciliatory the balance of power shifts and the barriers crumble. It is not uncommon that the secular feminist is made pregnant by a man who is all-too-ready to endorse equal rights for women—the woman is then left to fend for herself. In this way, an exploitative, materialistic man seeks to avoid responsibility and enjoy his senses.

On the other hand, a woman who pursues spirituality is protected by her discipline and the strictures of her religious tradition—she can never be exploited because she never engages in sinful activity. This separates her from her materialistic counterpart. What's more, she plays a leading and honored role within the social parameters of her family and community. Most importantly, she is devoted to God. She sees a spiritual equality—not a contrived material one. She feels that feminism betrays a narrow understanding of the purpose of existence, that it is predicated on competition between men and women. She knows that the only competition worth pursuing is between a person and his or her own conditioning. She has a role to play in her service to God, and it is this which concerns her—not some squabble about bodily differences.

But the big question revolves around how to determine which roles should be assigned to which individuals. Some feminists believe that this should be decided on a case-by-case basis, possibly asking each individual their opinion. Clearly, such a method would be an invitation to chaos. Therefore, all of the world's major religious traditions have assigned roles on the basis of individual differences built into creation. Men, generally endowed with more physical strength and thus a more aggressive nature, were given the forefront roles, while women, naturally endowed with domestic and maternal instincts, were given the supportive roles. Of course, this does not mean that *all* men are more aggressive than *all* women. But for the purposes of order and social sanity, the roles are assigned on the basis of the rule rather than the exception.

Recent scientific findings reveal that these roles are far from arbitrary. Studies conducted in some of America's most renowned universities, such as UCLA, UC Berkeley, and the University of Chicago, show beyond the shadow of a doubt that the functions and propensities of male and female brains are intrinsically different. *Science Digest* has been running a series of articles focusing on women and behavior, biochemistry, anatomy of the brain, and neuropsychology. In summary, these articles disclose that the brain is divided into two parts, the left and right hemispheres. Men are primarily controlled by the right hemisphere of the brain, while women are primarily controlled by the left. The left hemisphere has been found to specialize in language and memory, whereas the right hemisphere has been found to specialize in spatial reasoning. In other words, the natural propensities for men include mathematics, logic, construction, mechanics and military science, whereas women would be more inclined toward research, teaching, dictation, nursing, and paralegal work.

Interestingly, the activities pertaining to women require a great deal of patience, memory and language skills. This correlates with the *Bhagavad-gita*, wherein the inherent qualities of women were described centuries before the recent scientific findings, "speech, memory, intelligence, faithfulness and patience." (Bg. 10:34)

That men and women differ has been a well-observed fact from time immemorial. Unfortunately, these observations have traditionally led to the exploitation of women by materialistic men. Still if we learn how to *use* our differences in the service of God (rather than deny our differences for the purposes of sense gratification), we can simultaneously learn how to transcend these differences on a higher, spiritual platform.

Spiritually, the paradox is easily resolved. And now we have the help of science and technology. For instance, it has been found that light and sound accepted by the eye and ear, on one side of the head, are transmitted to the opposite side, or hemisphere, of the brain for processing. It was discovered that the right ear and eye are more sensitive in women, and the left in men. Also, the cortex, or the thinking part of the brain, has been found to be thicker on the left side for women, and on the right side for men. This does not diminish the quality of thinking for either party, but it does alter the propensities and preferences that may be naturally accepted or rejected by the cortex, making men and women psychologically different. Literally hundreds of such experiments are being conducted, and they continue to show evidence of differences between sexes of all species. And these differences correlate with the roles assigned to the various sexes by the world's religious literatures, particularly the Vedas.

Consequently, there is no basis for resentment on the part of any individual or group. Such resentment would simply reflect a selfish motivation, a search for sensual gratification divorced form life's ultimate goal. In the greater scheme of things, the design of God is best served by following the formula set down in the scriptures. Many great personalities—both men and women—have attained spiritual fulfillment by following the traditional methods; it is time-tested.

Nonetheless, in the feminists' quest for a perfectly egalitarian society, we find that nothing is sacred. Thus the National Council of Churches has recently released the "Inclusive Language Lectionary," a modernized translation of key Biblical passages. The Council, an organization of major Protestant denominations, apparently feels that masculine references to such eminent authority figures such as Jesus Christ and God offend the sensibilities of its distaff members. And so the new volume of Bible readings, meant to be used in public services, refers to God as "Sovereign One" rather than "Lord," and "Son of God" has been changed to "Child of God." This is a clear case of feminism running amok.

Is it really worth denying Jesus Christ's masculinity for the sake of linguistic neutrality? Many feminists think so. What can possibly be accomplished—on the spiritual platform—by calling him (him?!) the Child of God instead of the Son of God? Maybe the spiritual platform is not considered all that important in the realm of feminism. In any case, do we really have the right to tamper with established religious tradition because feminists prefer to read about an androgynous Christ?

There are instances where traditions can be changed—quite harmlessly—in order to accommodate modern, nonsexist views, even when they are only token gestures. For example, the National Weather Service avoided a storm of controversy several years ago when they began giving hurricanes and tropical tempests masculine as well as the traditional feminine names. Thus, we now have Tropical Storm Tommy as well as Hurricane Hilda, and meteorologists can no longer be accused of casting aspersions on the feminine temperament. But when feminists start looking skyward past those ominous clouds and gaze toward the heavens with an eye to "modify," then they'd better be ready for trouble. It's not nice to fool with Mother—er, *Parent* Nature.

In our search for perfect egalitarianism we are terribly afraid to admit that there are differences between sexes, or races, or nationalities, or humans of any group at all. Somehow the possibility that physical or psychological differences of any sort exist strike the fear that this will be equated with superiority or inferiority of certain groups. But the denial that differences exist, whether biological or otherwise, only leads to absurdities. Indeed, it is a denial of our own humanity. We cannot respect differences among people unless we first admit to them. This is not sexism or racism; it is merely common sense.

The most erroneous charge of modern-day feminists is that religion is sexist because it endorses the worship of a "male" God. This relatively new challenge to traditional faiths just confirms the view of some feminists that society has outgrown the need for religion. They agree with Freud and Marx that religions keep people dependent on authority and thwart their desire to improve their material situations.

Women with spiritual insight, however, are convinced that religion is profoundly important. For them, the discovery that religions seemingly teach the inferiority of women is sometimes experienced as a betrayal of deeply felt spiritual needs. They may come to believe that the history of sexism has permeated the human psyche but does not invalidate the human need for God, truth, and spirituality in general. Yet it may continually haunt them that God is viewed as "The Supreme Male."

For such women, the traditional religions of the West have, in a sense, betrayed them. Mainstream religions have neglected to teach that God, being Absolute, must have male as well as female manifestations—otherwise "Absolute" loses meaning. Everything is contained in the Absolute; anything that exists in this world has its prototype in the spiritual realm. Because male and female exist here, they also exist in God—but in perfection.

This is described to some degree in the mystical literature of the West, like the Kabbalah, but it is more elaborately discussed in the Vedic literature. Thus, women in general—and feminists in particular—should make careful note of the Vedas, for the female manifestation of God is therein described.

She is known as Shrimati Radharani, and She is the same as Krishna (the male manifestation of God). Yet She is eternally different as well. It is like the difference between the sun and the sunshine—they are inseparable and yet they are eternally separate. The sun is never actually the sunshine, nor can the sunshine really be called the sun. Yet you cannot have sunshine without the sun. One is the energy and the other is the energetic source. Clearly, these two are nondifferent. Without energy, there is no meaning to the energetic. What is the value of the sun without heat and light?

Similarly, without Radha, there is no meaning to Krishna, and without Krishna, there is no meaning to Radha. This is also the case in loving affairs: without the beloved, the lover feels useless, and vice-versa. Thus, in Vedic philosophy, the internal potency, Radharani, is given full respect, and She is glorified as the female aspect of the Absolute Truth.

In fact, She is worshipped *before* Krishna—They are referred to as Radha-Krishna. Even the *Maha-mantra, Hare Krishna, Hare Krishna, Krishna Krishna, Hare Hare/Hare Rama, Hare Rama, Rama, Rama, Hare Hare,* is a prayer first to Radha—*then* to Krishna. The word "Hare" is the vocative form of Mother Hara, another name for Shrimati Radharani. So the prayer is actually to Radha, the female manifestation of God: "O energy of the Lord. O Lord. Please engage me in Your service."

Even the Vedic literature, however, is reserved in telling us about Radharani. The Vedic sages knew that people would misconstrue the confidential truths of Radha-Krishna (possibly mistaking it for some mundane love affair), and they therefore describe them in very few places. The *Shrimad-Bhagavatam*, for instance, which is considered the most important Vedic work, only mentions Radharani in one obscure text (10:30:28) out of its mammoth eighteen thousand. And even then, She is mentioned with the oblique word *aradhita*, implying that She is the one special personality who has won Krishna's heart (although She is not really mentioned by name, nor is Her divinity fully described). The *Vishnu-purana* also alludes to Her existence. But She is clearly mentioned in other Vedic texts, such as the *Harivamsa*, and the *Naradiya, Padma, Brahmanda,* and *Brahma-vaivarta Puranas*, where the theology behind the female manifestation of God is fully developed. This may also be found in the commentaries of the great spiritual masters and in later Vedic works, such as *Gita-govinda* and the *Shri Chaitanya-Charitamrita*, the life story of Shri Chaitanya Mahaprabhu.

When Radha and Krishna unite it is called Chaitanya Mahaprabhu. This esoteric principle has a practical manifestation in the visible world. Lord Chaitanya appeared in India five hundred years ago to inaugurate the chanting of Hare Krishna as the means of self-realization in the present age. He was a combined manifestation of Radha and Krishna, and He delivered the essence of spiritual life. This, He taught, was embodied in the mood of the *gopis*, the village girls of Vrindavan who loved nothing but Krishna. Thus, the whole Vedic tradition exhorts all—men and women alike—to follow in the footsteps of the *gopis*, whose love for God remains unsurpassed. With the most elaborate spiritual tradition encouraging all living beings to follow the example of simple village girls (the *gopis*), and that same tradition giving a detailed explanation of God as the Supreme Female, what could stop a sincere feminist from giving herself totally to a life of God consciousness?

(A slightly revamped version of this essay appeared in the Premier issue (Vol. 1, No. 1, Winter 1988) of *Clarion Call Magazine*.)

20

WHOSE WORSHIP
IS IDOL WORSHIP?

Remember the old Cecil B. De Mille movies? The hero would rescue the innocent masses from the heathen idol worshipers by smashing the idols. And we would feel warm all over, our beliefs being molded as much by Hollywood as by Saturday or Sunday morning caterwaulers. We knew that the Bible condemned idol worship and, although we may not have been the most ardent religionists, we just knew that idol worship was wrong, as we continued to reverently watch our T.V. screen. Meanwhile, we adored Charlton Heston's version of Moses, Mr.Heston himself being the *idol* of millions.

What exactly is idol worship? Why is it condemned in the Bible? And who exactly is an idol worshiper? These are some of the questions we will address in the article. In the Bible, God exclaims, "Thou shalt have no other gods before me." (*Exodus* 20:3) This is the Lord's preface to His famous proscription of idol worship. And a significant preface it is. The implication is that the people of Israel were fashioning idols of entities other than God and worshiping them. The classic example is the golden calf. However, there is no restriction on worshiping *God's* image, but only on making an idol of "other gods." This is also a restriction in the so-called heathen scriptures. The Supreme Lord says in *Bhagavad-Gita,* the cream of ancient India's spiritual legacy, "Whatever a man may sacrifice to other gods is actually meant for Me alone—but it is offered without true understanding."

Now let us continue with the biblical statement against idol worship. "Thou shalt not make unto thee any graven (carved) image, or any likeness of any thing that is in the sky above, or that is on the earth beneath, or that is in the water under the earth....Thou shalt not bow down thyself to them, nor serve them: for I the Lord thy God am a jealous God..." (*Exodus* 20:4 and 5). Taking the Lord's preface into account and the last sentence of this verse, we can only conclude that His restriction is against making an image of a lesser god—for He is "a jealous God." We do ourselves an injustice when we take biblical texts out of context. It is evident that the Lord did not want the people of Israel to carve a form of some lesser god, which seemed to be their tendency (i.e.—the golden calf). But the Lord never says, "Do not carve a form of Me."

Obviously, His restriction was more against worshiping lesser gods than carving forms. Idol worpship means worshiping someone other than the Supreme Personality of Godhead.

But what if we could worship the form of the Supreme Lord? Would that be idol worship? Some may argue that the Lord is beyond form. They say that God is unlimited and can thus not be confined to some dimensional boundary. However, for God to be truly complete, as He must be by definition, He must also have a form. Otherwise, He is clearly incomplete. Everything in His creation has form, so how can God have no form? This would mean God is less than His creation—or in other words, that the complete is incomplete, which is simply illogical. The complete whole must contain everything within our experience and beyond our experience; otherwise He cannot be complete. In addition, all the great scriptures of the world instruct us to love God. How can we love something formless or void? It's impossible. We are all persons and we desire to love other persons—not some dark oblivion in outer space. We desire personal relationships, and the ultimate relationship is with the Supreme Personality of Godhead.

Granted, God's form is not like ours—it is completely transcendental—it is beyond the limitations of sense perception. But it is a form nonetheless. This is stated in one of the world's oldest religious literatures, the *Brahma-Samhita,*

isavarah paramah krsnah
sat-chid-ananda vigraha
anadir adir govinda
sarva karana karanam

"Krishna (God) is the Supreme Controller. He has a form made of eternity, knowledge, and bliss. He is the prime cause of all causes." (B.S. 5:1)

But religionists throughout the ages have projected their own limitations on the form of God. This is exemplified in the work of Moses Maimonides, the most respected biblical scholar of Medieval times, who stated in his *Mishna Torah* that God is said to be in the heavens above and on the earth below and could thus have no form. After all, Maimonides reasoned, one form cannot be in two places at once.

God may not have a form like Maimonides—a form that cannot be in two places at once—but that doesn't mean He has no form at all. In fact, He has an unlimited, transcendental form. And a close look at the biblical literature reveals this quite clearly, even though scholars such as Maimonides have relegated biblical statements about the form of God to the realm of metaphor. Still the Bible states: "Under His feet" (*Exodus* 24:10); "inscribed with the finger of God" (*Exodus* 31:18); "The hand of the Lord" (*Exodus* 9:3); "The eyes of the Lord" (*Genesis* 38:7); "The ears of the Lord" (*Numbers* 11:1), and other phrases such as these permeate the Biblical literature.

Why should the Bible be so misleading as to consistently present God as having a form if in reality He does not? This would be a dangerous metaphor, to be sure. Rather, the Bible clearly asserts that God *does* have a form, but that only the most qualified will ever get to see it, "Ye have neither heard His voice at any time nor seen His shape...Not that any man hath seen the Father, save he which is of God, he hath seen the Father." (*John* 5:37, 6:46)

In *Genesis*, chapters 18 and 19, God appeared before Abraham, the father of the nation of Israel. In this section of the Bible, God appears in a human-like form—although this form isn't elaborately described. Moses takes careful note of this manifestation. In verse one of chapter eighteen the Lord appeared to Abraham. In verse two, we are told that Abraham looked upon Him. In verse fourteen, while addressing Abraham, the Lord said of Himself, "Is anything too difficult for the Lord?" God's simple statement in this text defeats any skeptical idea as to whether or not He can have a form. He can do whatever He likes, and we shouldn't try to limit Him by saying "He can do this" and "He can't do that."

A similar phenomenon occurs again when God, in the form of a man, paid a nocturnal visit to Jacob on the bank of the Jabbok. In this encounter, Jacob came face to face with God (*Genesis* 32:24-32). Here the Bible is wonderfully reminiscent of Lord Krishna's pastime of wrestling with the cowherd boys of Vrindavan. Jacob is actually described as wrestling with someone who seems to be a man, eventually having his thigh dislocated by his heavenly adversary. The weary combatant in fact exclaimed that his opponent was in actuality the Supreme Lord. He memorialized the encounter by calling the place *Peniel*, which means "the face of God," and he exclaimed: "....I have seen God face to face, and my life is preserved" (*Genesis* 32:30). Some Bible translators render these texts differently, saying that Jacob saw "an angel" instead of God. This is because Judaism began to see God in an impersonal sort of way and could not recognize that Jacob had indeed seen "the face" of the Supreme Lord. However, the exact Hebrew word used in this connection is *Elohim*, which unmistakably refers to God Himself.

Moses was not to be denied the experience of perceiving this same form of God. Although it was Moses who related that no man can see God and live (*Exodus* 33:20), God did appear to him, and the Bible makes careful record of this. "Moses then went up with Aaron, Nadab, Abihu, and seventy elders of Israel, and they beheld the God of Israel." (*Exodus* 24:9 and 10). Subsequent texts indicate that Moses and the men were shocked, for they thought that sight of God meant instantaneous death. However, they all survived.

Moses obviously believed that he was standing in the presence of God Himself. In fact. Moses is elsewhere said to have seen the back of God (*Exodus* 33:23). If God can have a back, He can have a front. These terms have no meaning if God is simply an amorphous Being, with no form and no identity. And yet many biblical students opine that God is indeed formless. Of course, this impersonalistic theory not only goes against the original tradition of the Jews, but of Christians also. Every good Christian knows that Jesus sits at the Father's right hand. (*Mark* 16:19). Once again, the same logic—if He has a right hand, He has a left hand. Implicitly, God must have form.

And if this form were to be revealed by God's intimate devotees, or by God Himself, there is not a stricture in the world that says a lover of God cannot fashion a statue according to that image and worship it. After all, the form of God is not a thing of this world—it is not a "graven image of a lesser God in the sky, of the earth, or in the waters." In short, the Bible doesn't restrict us from worshiping God in His transcendental form—it only denounces cheap imitations (lesser gods). However, His actual form is another matter altogether. And since God's self-existent nature is absolute, He and His form are nondifferent. The worship of God in His original, transcendental form, as revealed by the pure devotee and by the scriptures, is called Deity worship—and it stands a long distance away from idol worship.

But the followers of the Western religious traditions have largely lost the sight of the form of God. Although the mystics of those traditions acknowledge that God does in fact have some spiritual form, even they are at loss when describing just what that form is. The Jewish mystics, for instance, say that God, in His heavenly Kingdom, complies with the commandments, wraps *tfillin* "around His arm," and wears a prayer shawl (*Rosh Hashanah* 17*b*, *Talmud*). They say that He even studies Torah three hours a day to set an example (*Aboda Zara* 3*b*, *Talmud*). Although most Jews are aware of these statements, they tend to make light of them, or once again, relegate them to the realm of metaphor.

Christians are certainly aware of God as a person. Jesus referred to God as *Abba*, Father, in a disarmingly personal way. So much so that the Jews of his time openly ridiculed him for it.

The mystics of Islam also declare that the form of God exists, while the orthodox, as in the other Occidental religions, deny it altogether. Still, one champion of orthodoxy, Al-Ashari (ninth century A.D.), declared in his creeds, "we confess that God has a countenance, without asking how...We confess that God has two hands, without asking why."

Thus, the mystics of all religious traditions acknowledge the form of God, albeit without detailed information. But ancient India's Vedic literature, which predates the Bible as well as the Koran, were written in a highly advanced spiritual culture, and they specifically reveal God's form, His features, His pastimes and His personality. Of course God's attributes are infinite, and words can only hint at HIs glory, but the Vedas supply man with more information than he can accommodate to the point of enlightenment. At that stage, man sees Krishna, God, everywhere, but that realization is very advanced and not to be imitated. And so the Vedas prescribe worship of the Deity of Krishna: we may not be able to see spirit—but we can see the Deity in the temple. This helps us to focus our minds on God—on His original form—until we are sufficiently pure to see Him spiritually. And once again, since the Lord is absolute, He is nondifferent from His Deity form in the temple. In this way, he purifies all on-lookers with His transcendental body.

The form of Krishna is vividly described in the Vedic literature, and His intimate, personal activities are narrated. Explicit details are given to carve Deities, not idols, in His Supreme Image. He may become jealous when we fashion some image of a lesser god, but He is pleased when we worship Him in His Deity form.

The form of Krishna—with his bluish hue, lotus eyes, blooming youthfulness, and pearl-white smile—is not fanciful. It is not an *image*, because it is not an *imagined*, or concocted form. It is not created by an artist, philosopher, or a mundane poet after seeing the beautiful panorama of the material world. This anthropomorphic idea doesn't answer the question, "Where does the beauty of nature come from?" Actually the beautiful things of nature are reflections of Krishna's original beauty. He is the prototype, as He explains in the *Bhagavad-gita* (10.41): "Know that all beautiful, glorious, and mighty creations spring from but a spark of My splendor." And Krishna's form is not anthropomorphic— rather, *our* form is theomorphic, fashioned after Krishna's form. We are made in the image of God. Now we might ask, "Why do you accept the statements in the Vedic literature about the form of God." But if we reflect for a moment, we can understand that every day we accept the statements of superior authorities on subjects we know nothing about. For instance, few of us have ever actually visited mainland China, yet we believe that it exists and that almost a billion people live there. We believe the magazine, newspaper, radio, and television reports about China and just about everything else. These are the sources of our knowledge, and if we wish we can confirm them by going to China ourselves, or by conducting independent investigation. In the same way, the Vedic literature is the source of knowledge that reveals Krishna's form to us. And we can confirm that knowledge as well—by following the Vedic teachings in our everyday life and developing the vision to see Krishna directly, beyond the Deity.

However, to properly receive the Vedic teachings we must approach a perfect authority, a person whose knowledge is coming from the Absolute through an unbroken line of spiritual masters. Then our knowledge will be perfect. His Divine Grace A.C. Bhaktivedanta Swami Prabhupada is such a spiritual master, and he has given us authoritative knowledge of Krishna's form through his translations of and commentary on *Bhagavad-gita As It Is*, *Shrimad-Bhagavatam*, and

Brahma-samhita. These books have existed more than five thousand years, and by following them many learned men and women have attained perfect knowledge of Krishna's existence.

For example, *Bramha-samhita* contains a detailed description of Krishna's body by one of the most exalted personalities in the universe, Lord Brahma. After thousands of years of meditation, Brahma actually met Krishna face to face. In his ecstasy he, unlike the biblical prophets, related what he saw, as best he could: "I worship Govinda, the primeval Lord, who is adept at playing on His flute, who has blooming eyes like lotus petals, whose head is bedecked with a peacock feather, whose figure of beauty is tinged with the hue of blue clouds, and whose unique loveliness charms millions of cupids. (Bs. 5.30).

"I worship Govinda, the primeval Lord, whose transcendental form is full of bliss, truth, and substantiality, and who is thus full of the most dazzling splendor. Each limb of that transcendental figure possesses in itself the full-fledged functions of all the other organs, and He eternally sees, maintains, and manifests the infinite universes, both spiritual and mundane" (Bs. 5:32).

Experts in the science of Krishna Consciousness have related to us the knowledge of Krishna's form through an unbroken line of disciplic succession. They encourage us to test the methods they prescribe, and to experience unlimited pleasure by seeing Krishna's form ourselves, first in the Deity, and then within every atom. Being based on experiment and observation, this, indeed, is ideal worship, not idol worship.

(This article originally appeared as a tract that was distributed in churches and universities throughout America. A slightly revised version appeared in *Clarion Call Magazine*, Vol. 1, No. 4, Autumn, 1988)

21

THE AGNI AND
THE ECSTASY

uly 10, 1975. It was a beautiful summer day. Although I was an exuberant twenty-year-old, I had no qualms about staying indoors on this occasion. I was being initiated into the ancient tradition of Krishna consciousness by my spiritual master, His Divine Grace A.C. Bhaktivedanta Swami Prabhupada, the founder-*acharya* of the International Society for Krishna Consciousness.

I had been working toward this for some time. When I joined the movement in 1973, my intention was to make a short experiment. I had just read Mahatma Gandhi's autobiography, *Experiments With Truth*, and I romanticized how I would experiment in a similar way.

Also, just before joining the movement, I had read Irving Stone's *Agony and the Ecstasy*, a fictionalized account of Michelangelo's life. I was fascinated by the great Renaissance man's resolve to paint the Sistine Chapel upon the request of Pope Sixtus IV. Michelangelo's work as a painter for the Pope necessitated a mood of surrender, for he considered himself primarily a sculptor.

I fancied myself something other than a devotee of God. I was a musician, an artist, and somewhat of a scholar. So I considered myself a sort of Renaissance man in my own right. But through reading Shrila

Prabhupada's profound works—translations of and commentaries on the ancient Vedic literature—I came to understand what I really wanted to pursue: God's mission in this world.

Before coming to Krishna consciousness, I had read that religion originated in the East. *Yoga* groups and meditation centers back in America, while popular, did not satisfy my urge for a way of life that was completely spiritual. I took a short trip to India but returned dissatisfied. Traditional Hinduism seemed too dogmatic, with its many gods and family-based caste distinctions. Nonetheless, I knew Hinduism had its roots in the Vedic literature, and I became interested in this source of spiritual truth.

Knowing that the Vedas were written in Sanskrit, I decided to enroll in a Sanskrit course at Queens College in New York. If I could learn the language, I reasoned, then I could interpret the texts for myself, and I didn't have to rely on the commentaries of popular *yogis* and *swamis.*

My professor was using Shrila Prabhupada's *Bhagavad-gita As It Is.* I had read many editions of the *Gita,* but only after reading Shrila Prabhupada's version was I aware that Krishna is God Himself and that the plurality of gods for which Hinduism is so famous is a fairly recent innovation. For me, this was an important revelation: the religion upon which Hinduism rests is strongly monotheistic!

I was also surprised that caste distinction as interpreted by the British—and most Hindus—has little to do with what is actually taught in the Vedic texts. While the popular misconception holds that one fits into a specific caste according to birthright, the Vedas—and especially the *Bhagavad-gita*—teach that one's quality and work determine one's social position. A person is considered a *brahmana,* for instance, by virtue of his being an intellectual, not because he is born to a *brahmana* father. This is clear from the Sanskrit texts themselves. So my Sanskrit course helped me to see the logic of the Vedic literature and the accuracy of Prabhupada's translation and commentary.

More important for me, however, was the realization that Prabhupada was not only delivering *Bhagavad-gita* "as it is," but was indeed espousing original Vedic culture as it is. I knew this was what I had been looking for.

As I became more familiar with the Sanskrit language and the ancient Vedic tradition to which it belongs, I became convinced of Shrila Prabhupada's authenticity. I felt compelled to visit his Hare Krishna center in New York City, which was listed in the back of my *Bhagavad-gita.*

Luckily, on a rainy spring day in 1973, Shrila Prabhupada was lecturing at the Henry Street temple in Brooklyn. It was my first visit to the temple, and although Shrila Prabhupada was always travelling, he was there on that day. I understand now that this arrangement was Krishna's mercy on me, because being quite a skeptic, no one short of Shrila Prabhupada himself could have convinced me of the validity of Krishna consciousness.

Although I came with a battery of questions regarding metaphysical reality and ontological truth, I didn't walk away disappointed. I was astounded by Shrila Prabhupada's lecture. Without my asking, he had answered all my questions—and then some!

Still I maintained a healthy skepticism. The scriptures advise that one apply logic and reason in the pursuit of truth. So for a full year I studied Shrila Prabhupada's books closely, visited the temple, and asked questions. I adopted the basic principles of Krishna consciousness: I started chanting the Hare Krishna *maha-mantra* on beads every day, and I avoided meat-eating, illicit sex, intoxication, and gambling.

Seeking happiness, I had formerly indulged in all of these activities. But somehow, I knew, true happiness was eluding me, no matter how successful I was in enjoying my senses. In retrospect, I think that my prior indulgence served to reinforce my current resolve, for despite my sensual gratification, I had become less and less happy. Although I was engaging in sinful life to numb the pain of material existence, it just wasn't working. Rather, I was becoming more and more entangled. The very activities I thought were bringing me pleasure and freedom were actually the source of my misery and bondage. I was embracing as the cure that which causes the disease.

In the beginning I faltered quite a bit. But as I became more steady in following the basic rules, I could feel my consciousness becoming purified. It gradually became easier to lead a purer life. Nonetheless, although things were becoming "easier," they were still a challenge, and I didn't know if I had what it takes to make a lifetime commitment. Despite this period of uncertainty, however, my experiments became more and more serious.

In 1974, I saw Shrila Prabhupada lecture at the Ratha-yatra (Festival of the Chariots) in San Francisco. After the lecture, Shrila Prabhupada sang and danced with the devotees in glorification of God. He was happy and deeply absorbed in transcendent reality, and everyone who watched him knew it. Here, I thought, is someone who practices what he preaches.

This event solidified my faith in the process of Krishna consciousness. I knew then and there that Shrila Prabhupada was my spiritual guide and that I would one day be initiated by him. Whatever my reservations, I knew I had to make a commitment. If I didn't, I would be selling myself short.

As I became a more dedicated follower, I went out and distributed Shrila Prabhupada's books on a daily basis. I wanted to share this treasure that had somehow been bestowed upon me. To this end, I joined the Shri Shri Radha-Damodar Sankirtan Party, a team of devotees who were absorbed in distributing Prabhupada's literature and message to the world.

February 28, 1975 was a cold day in Atlanta, Georgia. We had travelled there to meet Shrila Prabhupada, who was arriving from a successful lecture tour of Caracas and Miami. I was one of some three hundred enthusiastic devotees—both old and new—who were there to greet Prabhupada. Although many of us were uninitiated, we had made a serious commitment, and there was talk that initiations would be forthcoming, perhaps six months away.

For the next four days, we heard Prabhupada lecture every morning, expounding the basic philosophy of Krishna consciousness with unexcelled clarity and precision. Prabhupada knew that his explanations of the fundamentals would help his young novices preach to those whom they would meet on book distribution. By hearing Prabhupada explain the fundamentals in such a masterful way, I developed confidence in my own ability to convey these same truths to others.

During those early-morning winter lectures in Atlanta, an interesting phenomenon would occur on a daily basis: As I wanted to develop a more intimate relationship with Shrila Prabhupada, I would plan out several deep philosophical questions before his lecture. I had hoped that after his talks I would have the opportunity to ask these questions and revel in the spiritual exchange. Without my asking, however, he would invariably answer my questions during his lecture. Sometimes I would even purposely think of questions that had no relation to the daily topic. But these questions were always answered.

By the fourth day, I was certain that this was more than mere coincidence. I was confident that, as my spiritual master, he knew my mind even better than I. As if in confirmation of this, after his lecture, he turned to me (I was sitting only a few feet away!) and said, "Are all questions answered?"

In response, I sat there with my mouth hanging open. Of course, it was not uncommon for him to say this at the end of his lectures, but in this instance he looked right into my eyes. It was fully appropriate, and for me it had very special meaning.

Before Shrila Prabhupada was to leave Atlanta and we were to continue our travels throughout the country distributing his books, Tamal Krishna Goswami, the leader of our party, asked Shrila Prabhupada if he would like to meet each of us. Wanting to give us special encouragement, Shrila Prabhupada agreed.

Though I had seen Prabhupada on several occasions, regularly listened to his tapes, and carefully studied his books, this would be the first time I would actually *meet* him. I was nervous and excited. While this meeting would be important and certainly pleasurable in many ways, I knew that it would deepen my commitment to the spiritual path. That prompted a sense of fear. Was I ready? The "agony and the ecstasy" motif entered my mind. Michelangelo wanted to sculpt, but in surrendering to the will of the Pope he had sculpted a new life for himself as a painter.

My eternal spiritual father, whom I had acknowledged as such for a mere two years, was now going to enter my life in a more intimate and personal way. As our Radha-Damodara Party literally danced through the door to his room singing the names of Krishna, I felt our relationship deepen—all of us as Godbrothers under our spiritual father, Shrila Prabhupada.

One after another we were introduced to Prabhupada. We each offered him a fragrant flower, which he graciously accepted, and then we offered our prostrated obeisances. Prabhupada smiled with great delight as Tamal Krishna Goswami explained to him our respective services.

"This is Tom," Tamal Krishna Goswami said. "He fixes the buses in which the devotees travel." Prabhupada nodded approvingly. "This is Danny. He does the cleaning. Mike assists with the cooking. Bob distributes your books..."

"Oh?" Prabhupada interrupted. "This is *very* nice!" It was clear that Prabhupada had a preference for seeing his books distributed. All other services were valuable in that they assisted this one service of transmitting transcendental knowledge and love of God.

I was up next. Also a book distributor, I felt somewhat confident that Prabhupada would be pleased with my service. "This is Steve," said Tamal Krishna Goswami, "and he distributes your books as well." No reaction. As I went to offer him the flower, I realized that the same phenomenon had occurred again. Since he had just expressed his delight with the previous book distributor, there was no need to say anything new to me. It was just like his answering my questions before I asked them.

Still, after a few moments, Prabhupada looked up at me with folded hands and said, "Thank you very much." I immediately felt a spiritual reciprocation I had never felt before. He appreciated my service. And I appreciated his encouragement. In that moment I realized that I was in the presence of my spiritual father and eternal well-wisher.

Four months passed. We were travelling throughout the U.S. delivering the message of Krishna consciousness. It was early July, and we were told that Prabhupada would meet us in Chicago to formally initiate those of us who were true to our vows. Seventy-five young devotees would now strengthen their link with the Vedic tradition through the holy rite of initiation, and then we would all attend the 1975 Festival of the Chariots in Chicago.

Again we spent many mornings listening to Prabhupada lecture from *Shrimad Bhagavatam.* This time several hundred devotees gathered in the huge hall of the Evanston temple. Prabhupada took this opportunity to expound on the life of Ajamila, a sinful person who at the time of death had saved himself by calling out the name of God: "Narayana! Narayana!"

Prabhupada enjoyed telling this story, for here the power of the holy name comes across powerfully. Ajamila had named his son Narayana, a name for God, and at the time of death Ajamila called out for the boy with full sincerity. Because he called the name of Narayana, he was saved from death and was given the chance to attain spiritual perfection. "Just see," said Shrila Prabhupada. "This is the potency of the holy name." Even if chanted inadvertently, it has tremendous effect."

On the fourth day of Prabhupada's Chicago lectures, another miracle occurred. After repeating Narayana's name many times in telling the story of Ajamila, Shrila Prabhupada fell into trance. This was something he rarely did in public. An intense silence engulfed the room. We all felt blessed to witness this transcendental phenomenon. Through purely calling out Narayana's name, Prabhupada was seeing Narayana face to face. His trance-like state and his inability to speak lasted two minutes. Although I had read about the ecstatic symptoms of a pure devotee, I was amazed to see them. Those of us who were in the room will never forget his spiritually uplifting expression.

After two seemingly eternal minutes, Shrila Prabhupada said, "All right. Thank you very much." Then he gestured that *kirtan* [group chanting] should begin, and one of the most intense chanting sessions I had ever experienced permeated the large hall.

Then came the initiation. Anticipation filled my heart. My imagination went wild. I pictured sages in ancient times taking part in similar ceremonies on the banks of India's holy rivers. Now I would have the good fortune to follow in their footsteps. I looked forward to the exotic and colorful initiation ceremony, which includes a purificatory fire sacrifice. I had imagined this in my mind's eye for months. The room would be filled with smoke from the flames of the ancient Vaishnava ceremony. I was familiar with the initiation procedure, for I had several months earlier been to the initiation of my senior Godbrothers. Each initiate would come before Shrila Prabhupada, who would give him or her a set of chanting beads and a spiritual name. This name is usually one of the names of Krishna (or one of His eternal associates) followed by the word "*dasa*" (for men) or "*devi-dasi*" (for women), both of which mean "servant." The name reminds the disciple that he or she is a servant of God.

Now my own initiation was about to take place. Shrila Prabhupada started calling the devotees one by one. There were seventy-five of us, so my fear was alleviated by the fact that I was not alone. Still, the agony-and-the-ecstasy concept ran through my mind as I thought of the sacrificial fire soon to be ignited. My entire life up to the point of initiation ran before my eyes. Knowing that in Sanskrit the fire is called *agni-hotra*, I started to play mental word games: "The *agni* and the ecstasy," I thought. This was not a time to play games, however, and I made an internal promise to be more serious.

The fire at such sacrifices is always a marvelous thing to behold. In this particular situation, however, I had mixed feelings. On the one hand, I could hardly wait for Shrila Prabhupada to call my name, so we could get on with the beautiful fire sacrifice. On the other hand, I was as nervous as hell! The commitment of life-long dedication is frightening. But I knew that one can get out of Krishna consciousness only what one is ready to put into it. I had made up my mind.

To ease the tension, I enjoyed watching several of Prabhupada's senior disciples spread colored dyes over the dirt mound in decorative crisscrosses just prior to the sacrifice. "What is actually being sacrificed?" I began to ask myself. Surely it was mainly my false ego, my false sense of proprietorship. I was now acknowledging that I am not God but, rather, His blissful servant.

"Ah, to be a servant of God," I thought, "—this is no ordinary thing."

No sooner was I thinking in this way than I heard someone call out my name. It was Tamal Krishna Goswami. He was calling me forward to be initiated by Shrila Prabhupada. I took a deep breath and approached Prabhupada's seat. As he handed me the beads, he said, "Do you know the four rules?"

"Yes," I answered. "No intoxication, no illicit sex, no meat-eating, and no gambling." I had been practicing what to say so I wouldn't muff it. The four rules are easy enough to remember, but less easy to follow. And when you're nervous, they're even hard to remember!

"Correct," Prabhupada said. "Follow these four principles and chant a minimum of sixteen rounds on your beads everyday. Hare Krishna." Then the moment I had been waiting for: "Your name is Satyaraja."

I immediately looked over at one of my traveling mates who knew Sanskrit better than I. "It means 'king of truth,'" he said. I looked back at Prabhupada with a sense of pride. Yes, this is me—I am the king of truth!

Prabhupada looked at me squarely in the eyes and reminded me of the handy little affix: "Dasa!"

I felt two inches tall. Here I was trying to remember that the real sacrifice was the sacrifice of my false ego, and Prabhupada had shown me, by pausing before saying "dasa," that I was still anxious to think of myself as something special. In short, I was inadvertently trying to be an imitation God. Prabhupada had lectured many times explaining that this in fact is the very reason for our material existence: the endeavor to replace the Lord and be the central enjoyer of all we survey. Prabhupada taught me a valuable lesson at the initiation by reminding me that I was merely a humble servant of "the king of truth."

As I walked away from his seat with my beads and new name— Satyaraja dasa—I also walked away from the agony-and-the-ecstasy concept. The agony, I realized, was merely a product of my own rebellion against God. Now, through Prabhupada's grace, I realized that I am constitutionally a servant of God. So the agony was gone. As I watched the sacrificial fire burn away, I knew that all that was left was ecstasy.

(This article originally appeared in *Back to Godhead Magazine*, Vol. 24, No. 7.)